The MAGIC Within

Synchronicity & Other Miracles

By
NANCY STROUPE

MMXXI

The Magic Within: Sunchronicity & Other Miracles

Copyright © 2021 by Nancy Stroupe.
All rights reserved.

It is illegal to copy, distribute, or create derivative works from this book in whole or in part or to contribute to the copying, distribution, or creating of derivative works of this book.

No portion of this book may be reproduced, stored in a retrieval system, or transmitted in any form or by any means—electronic, mechanical, photocopying, recording or otherwise—without written permission from the publisher.

Photographs, cover design and copy by Nancy Stroupe
    and Danica De La Mora
Cover image, book design and layout by Danica De La Mora

Published by Timeless Treasures Publishing
P.O. Box 278
Crossnore, NC 28616
www.TimelessTreasuresStudio.net
info@TimelessTreasuresStudio.net

Available from Amazon.com.
Also available on Kindle and other devices.

First edition: March, 2021.

Paperback ISBN: 978-1-953940-07-0
Hardcover ISBN: 978-1-953940-09-4
Kindle ISBN: 978-1-953940-08-7

Manufactured in the United States of America.

Disclaimer: This book details the author's personal experiences with and opinions about synchronicity and other topics. This book is not to be used to treat any medical or emotional condition. For those issues, please consult a licensed healthcare practitioner.

DEDICATION

This book is dedicated to all of these wonderful people who joined me in my stories of synchronicity and other miracles. All of you have played such important roles in my life at various times and without you my stories would not have been possible.

This book also is dedicated to my wonderful and talented daughter, Danica De La Mora, who did the layout, designed a truly remarkable and eye-catching cover, and encouraged me while she was writing her own great books.

Additionally, this book is dedicated to my husband, Bruce Morrison, who continues to reside in a skilled nursing home setting with nearly impossible visitation, thanks to COVID-19. Bruce, I promise, the next book I finish will be the one you started!

DANICA DE LA MORA   BRUCE MORRISON

Foreword

Do I believe in miracles? You bet I do! After living the life I have where incredible miracles and other almost unbelievable events have happened on such a regular basis, how could I not? So come share my adventures. Perhaps you will find inspiration and hope that we are not alone and that the universe is guided by a kindly hand that watches over each of us and sends us just what we need when we need it!

Some of you who have read my first book, *One Column At A Time*, will find several of the same stories in this book, although they have been expanded and more details added. I actually got the idea for this book when I was writing the stories for the *Columns* book. I had already started a book about miracles and other odd and inspirational happenings in life and I suddenly realized I had a lot of true stories that would serve as examples of the concepts I was presenting. So, I decided to combine them and to add many more examples that are mostly from my own life with a few added from other people.

We all need hope, inspiration, and our very own bits of magic sprinkled through our lives. Without the magic and the possibility of more magic in the future, life becomes dull and disenchanting. I hope these stories will inspire you to notice and appreciate the real magic in your own life.

Look for the accompanying *The Magic Within Journal*. It is a good place to record your own personal miracles, your dreams, and the things for which you are grateful.

I do hope you enjoy!

Nancy
March, 2021

Contents

Chapter 1: Finding Your Fairy Godmother 1
Chapter 2: Your Place in the Universe 5
Chapter 3: A Tale of Synchronicity 13
Chapter 4: What is Synchronicity Anyway? 16
Chapter 5: The Bandleader's Vision 18
Chapter 6: Oktoberfest Phenomenon 23
Chapter 7: Psychic Synchronicity 27
Chapter 8: Synchronicity on the Cascade Loop 30
Chapter 9: Synchronicity at the Falls 34
Chapter 10: Synchronicity in a Small World 36
Chapter 11: Inspirational Synchronicity 39
Chapter 12: Synchronicity from My Childhood 42
Chapter 13: Myles Standish Revisited 46
Chapter 14: A Synchronistic Tale of Two Flat Tires 51
Chapter 15: Synchronicity Stops a Con Artist 56
Chapter 16: Chance Question Synchronicity 66
Chapter 17: Manifesting 71
Chapter 18: A Little Manifesting of My Own 77
Chapter 19: Manifesting a Husband 80
Chapter 20: Gratitude 87

Chapter 21: Be Careful What You Wish For 89

Chapter 22: The Nature of the Universe 93

Chapter 23: Lucid Dreams 96

Chapter 24: Miracle in a Snowstorm..................................... 101

Chapter 25: Random Synchronicities 104

Chapter 26: More Small Miracles 113

Chapter 27: A Few More Stories.. 122

Chapter 28: Unexplainable Connections 136

Chapter 29: Messages from Beyond...................................... 142

Chapter 30: Time 146

Chapter 31: Making Postulates.. 153

Chapter 32: Guided Meditation 158

Chapter 33: Out of Body Experiences.................................. 166

Chapter 34: Negative Energy & Thoughts 170

Chapter 35: Trusting Your Intuition... 174

Chapter 36: Been There, Done That!.................................... 179

Chapter 37: Using Affirmations to Help Create Your World 182

Chapter 38: The Magic Within 184

Recommended Reading List 188

1

Finding Your Fairy Godmother

I must have been about eight when I realized, in one blistering moment of clarity, that my fairy godmother would not be showing up one day to grant me three wishes. Up until that day, I had spent at least some of my time planning just what I would wish for when she appeared.

I was sitting on the grass in my yard in the mountains. It was a beautiful day in mid-summer and I could smell the white blooms in the clover around me. I was indulging in my game of "when my fairy godmother grants me three wishes, the first one will be 'I wish every wish I wish will come true.'"

Suddenly, it dawned on me that my game was just that, a game, a fantasy in my head, and that nothing magical would happen out there in the real world. Actually, it seemed to me that the beautiful summertime colors of nature underwent a major change in that instant and everything looked a dull gray. I know the sunshine seemed to leave. Or maybe I just remember it that way, because it took a lot of years before I discovered the magic again.

Perhaps that last paragraph is a little misleading. I think I always realized that there were small moments scattered through my life that seemed magical and very much out of the ordinary.

There were the **coincidences** or incidents of **synchronicity**. How many times have you thought of someone only to have that person call you shortly? Have you ever waked up thinking of someone and run into him a short time later when you had not seen him in months? I'm am sure you have had the experience of trying to think of a word and then seeing or hearing it as soon as you stopped trying so hard to think of it. We will talk more about coincidences later and how you can increase their occurrences in your everyday life.

The majority of the true stories in this book contain elements of synchronicity. Sometimes it seems to me that the world operates on synchronicity. These "chance" coincidences bring the most extraordinary things and events into our lives.

Some of the other "miracle" stories I am recounting here deal with **manifesting**, which is the art of bringing into physical form whatever you hope to attain or achieve. There have been many books written on the subject of bringing those things you want into your life. I certainly have been able to manifest things on a number of occasions.

There were the times when I experienced moments of *déjà vu*, or the feeling that I had been to a place in the past when I knew that I had not. Sometimes I knew exactly what someone was going to say before he said it, and even whole conversations occasionally. At other times, my actions were so achingly familiar that I could hardly believe I had never done what I was doing before and I have even been homesick for places I have never been!

I certainly cannot omit **postulates** and their effects when discussing the magic we can find surrounding us daily. In fact, the concept of postulates is so important that I have devoted a chapter to it later in the book. Have you ever wanted something badly and found that it came to you in a way you had never considered would happen? Or have you hoped something would occur and, to your surprise, it did? We all have known people who had a dream and focused their lives toward making their dream come true. Many of us wonder why we are unable to do such a thing ourselves, don't we?

Another strange and changing concept is **time** itself. Time flows in starts and stops. Seriously. An hour spent in the dental chair is not the same amount of time as an hour spent relaxing with friends and enjoying the company and the conversation, is it? Have you noticed that time speeds up as you get older? And sometimes, time does not act the way it should. Sometimes time and reality get tangled up and both seem warped!

The concept of **reality** does seem to be linked up with the concept of time. We all like to think that reality is the same for all of us. But after working in the field of mental health, I can tell you it most assuredly is not! I would go even further to say that reality is not really the same for any of us. But how do we know? We can't even know if we perceive the same colors. Red might be very different for you than it is for me.

Intuition, or our "sixth sense," is that ability to understand or discern without conscious reasoning. We tease and make jokes about "women's intuition," but what if it is real? Have you ever just known something, but had no idea how you knew? Have you had strong feelings about a decision with no logical idea why that was the case?

Have you ever had a **lucid dream**? A lucid dream is one in which you are aware that you are dreaming while it is occurring. Many times, you can control what takes place in the dream or choose what to do just like in your awakened state. Lucid dreams offer all kinds of chances to experiment with our imagination and our concept of the universe.

A technique that many life coaches and New Age philosophers tend to use a lot involves **affirmations**. I have helped several people set up and use affirmations to deal with their real life problems and we will talk more about the technique later in the book.

Another technique employed is that of **guided meditation**. It is much llike traditional meditation in that it helps one to relax, to reduce stress and anxiety, and to produce more energy of a positive nature. I will give you several examples of guided meditation in a later chapter.

Then there are the **out of body experiences** or OBEs. There are many people who claim they have had such experiences. Could they be real?

I personally think most suicides occur when the person has decided the "magic" is over for him and the future holds no hope that anything special ever will happen to him again.

If you are wondering why I am starting this book with a discussion of magic, I can say only that life is truly magic, you are capable of great feats of magic, and I want to give you inspiration to help you use your own special powers of magic to enrich and guide your life.

Over the years, I have been exposed to and/or investigated many techniques and philosophies that claimed to make lives far better and increase abilities and powers. Some disciplines had some merit. Others were shams, taking large sums of money from people who were seeking various forms of salvation. Some of the disciplines and philosophies I have had some exposure to or participated in have been psychology, ESP and paranormal phenomena, Taoism, mysticism, existentialism, Judaism, Christianity, Scientology, metaphysics, Native American culture and spiritual beliefs, past life regression, and more. I found kernels of truth and helpfulness here and there in each of them. I also found much that I could not possibly agree with and those things I did not keep. I found that the more I studied, the more eclectic I became.

In my career as a therapist, I finally decided that I could do more good by helping people believe in themselves and trust their own feelings than in doling out platitudes in the latest psychological jargon and terminology.

We all need some magic in our lives. And magic is woven all throughout my stories. I hope you will enjoy taking a trip into the extraordinary with me and will find your own magic to brighten your days and give you hope and optimism for the future.

2

Your Place in the Universe

We hold the only key to our own happiness.
We must unlock our own doors and find our own way.

From the time we are small, our primary occupation seems to be trying to place ourselves comfortably somewhere in the overall scheme of things. You probably would not be reading this book if you were not trying to understand yourself and your options better. Psychiatrists' and psychologists' offices are filled with people trying to "find themselves." I suppose one could say that our institutions for the mentally ill are filled with the unfortunate people who were not successful in doing so to any meaningful degree.

The majority of us finally reach some conclusions with which we can live, even though we haven't really figured things out. We consciously decide that the universe is a very mysterious place and it is not possible to understand it. At that point, many of us make a "leap of faith" and decide to leave it up to our concept of God to handle the rest of it, because we believe we cannot see the overall picture. All of our many churches did not just happen. They came into existence to fill our very real need to feel anchored to something steady and to be cared for by someone who can see everything, know everything, and control everything.

At birth, many of us ruled our world. All we had to do was open our mouths and we had food and comfort. In addition to the nourishment and the warm, dry diaper and clothes, we usually had our own "slave" who cuddled us and tried to make sure we were happy in every way. Some of us even had two of these "servants" who played with us, read to us, cleaned up every spill, carried us around, and tried to give us many new learning experiences. These people, of course, are normally called "parents"!

We knew our place in the universe at that point. We were the center and everything else was here for the sole purpose of seeing to our needs. **We were important**. But gradually it dawned on us that our caregivers were trying to turn the tables and make us do what they wanted. Many of us spent our first several years fighting to keep our dominant position intact. Everything became a battle. From potty training to feeding ourselves, we fought against having to do what we were told. We wanted to call the shots. We wanted to do the things that interested us. We definitely did not want to be controlled by our former slaves!

It was rather surprising to see the lengths some of these parents were willing to go in order to gain our cooperation. They bribed us, they tricked us, they coerced us, and if all else failed, they threatened us. Even if we came from homes where there was at least one abusive parent, we soon learned just where the limits were. We knew how far to push or when to pretend to be invisible and when to be really absent if we could.

During the way, we discovered an amazing fact: **the universe could hurt you if you didn't watch out!** If we didn't yield, objects in our path could leave major bumps and bruises. We could get burned with fire or heat, and cold wasn't very pleasant, either. Glass and sharp objects could cut or scratch us. Our earliest perception of steps seemed to be from lying at the bottom after a fall. Even a few tentative steps could result in a major upset. Our world, as it expanded, changed from the safest, surest of places to an insecure, unknown territory that could be terrifying at times.

On a subconscious level, we began to question our position sometime during this period. Our relationship with our parents was changing. There were new demands and, if we did not meet them, the consequences could be quite unpleasant. More and more we began to view ourselves as "the little guy" and our parental figures as "the big guys."

As our knowledge of the world grew, our control over it lessened.

At some point, we found ourselves no longer the ruling centers of our universe; we found ourselves dependent on the adults in our world for all of our security. Most of us can remember being afraid to leave our parents for any length of time. At least with them, we had learned that certain actions could be counted upon to bring certain responses. Other "little guys" had parents who were a bit different from ours. Our tantrums or tears, strangely, did not produce exactly the same results they did at home. And, many times, these parental figures did not have as much patience or caring as did our own parents.

Soon, school became a micro-world for us. We tested our power, our popularity, and our abilities in many ways. We were **students**. This institution was our focus for most of these early years. We took our self-image that we had formed with our family in our preschool years and modified and expanded it in order to cope in the scholastic environment. How successful we were in school depended to a large degree on how well we were able to adapt to this structured setting. Our job was learning. We had ups and downs, of course, but most of us will remember our secondary schooldays as some of our most secure times. We knew what grade we were in. If we listened in class, we knew what was expected of us. We were aware of what would happen if we talked in class or if we failed to do our homework. We usually knew when tests were coming and knew when to study the hardest. We knew when vacations were and we looked forward to weekends when we could give up all the responsibility for a while and just play.

Perhaps we did not like our perceived place in our class and our homes, but we didn't do a lot of floundering or wondering who we were at this point in our lives. Many of us were also learning in our churches. Sunday "schools" usually attempted to teach children their place in the universe in relation to God. Just as there were rules at home and in school, there were rules in religion.

Early on, most children bought these rules and didn't entertain thoughts of questioning them. There were good and bad experiences with church. Some religions offered comfort and hope, while others taught a doctrine laced with fear of a punitive God who meted out harsh punishments if strict guidelines were not followed. We saw God as a wonderful, nurturing "super parent" watching over us with loving help, or as a "super cop" making hard-to-follow rules and evoking swift justice if we did not do so—or as something in between.

Gradually, we became aware of occurrences in the world around us that didn't fit in with our concept of God. How could the warm, caring God allow the horrible suffering we saw around us? Or why did some criminals continually get by with their crimes, even when people knew they were being committed. Why didn't our strict adherence to "right deeds" always bring us a pleasant life?

So we tried to reconcile the differences in various ways. Perhaps we decided we needed the suffering to enable us to grow and to make us appreciate the good things in life. Or perhaps we thought the people who did wrong with no sign of punishment would get their just rewards at God's hands after their deaths.

But most of us finally stopped really trying to figure out God and precepts of religion. We just trusted that things were working as they should and, if we could see the overall scheme of things, we would find that everything had a reason for happening as it did. This conclusion was easier to live with than constant questioning and re-examining of the world.

I think it is important to note that most self-concepts are formed by perceived reflection. That is, we constantly evaluate how other people respond to us and we judge how we must look in their eyes. In formative stages, insults and belittlements from others can have devastating results in our own opinion of ourselves.

Nowhere is this formation process more obvious than in adolescence. Many teenagers judge themselves on how closely they conform to their peer group's ideas of beauty, behavior, and success. It is such an emotional time. The hormones are trying to prepare the body to adjust to all the responsibilities of adulthood and it is a big adjustment. It is hard to pick up a magazine that does not have at least one article about the problems of coping with your teenager and his or her disruptive behavior. Today's young person has a harder struggle with the self-concept that ever before. I attribute this increased difficulty to a number of things, including a less stable family unit and the subtly invasive media.

A few years ago, my own child was an adolescent and I spent some time watching the shows she favored. The nation's foremost children's channel had a great selection of the old favorites in the evenings. However, in the afternoons, almost every presentation cast derision at the adults in the show. There was the high school principal who was stupid and mean and could always be outsmarted by the kids in the end. There were the parents who were bunglers and who never caught on to what the very intellectual kids were planning. There was the camp counselor who had to be avoided if any scheme was to succeed. There was the employer who was less than average in I.Q. and could be counted on for a good laugh at the hands of his teenage employees. Smart kids, stupid adults was the message. Should it have come as any surprise that most kids loved this channel? It imparted a concept of "kid power" many of them didn't have in their own families. It also should not have been surprising when our children didn't accord us the respect that we gave our own parents.

By the time we have finished school, we have come to terms, for the most part, with our self-concept. We set out to live our lives based on what we perceive are our major skills and talents. We believe some areas of life are closed to us because we don't have the abilities or desires they would require. And so we go on, some to more education, some to marriage and families, others to menial jobs, and still we wonder.

Maybe I should amend my last statement and say that some of us wonder. Years ago when I was a therapist at an alcoholism treatment center in the southeast, I came to the conclusion that some of us really don't wonder.

I was sitting in the records department looking up a chart I needed when I overheard two of the secretaries discussing what they were going to fix for supper as though that were the most pressing concern of their lives. I suddenly realized that I had heard this same topic discussed many times by these same two ladies. I tried to remember just what else I had heard them discuss over the several years I had known them. Such things as church services and who preached, who had died complete with when and cause, relatives coming to visit or them visiting relatives, who got divorced, and painting or wallpapering rooms in their houses came to mind. I couldn't remember ever hearing anything discussed other than very concrete aspects of their everyday lives.

When I realized that perhaps their world was limited to these types of things, I had to stop and see how content they were with their "place in the universe." They never seemed to have any major worries. I would have found their lives quite boring, I think, but they did not.

When I asked them why they never discussed where life in general was heading, what their purpose in life was, and other questions I seemed to spend much time on, they looked at me as though I had grown another head! They informed me that God made the universe and He knew what was best for all of us and we didn't need to concern ourselves with anything of that nature. Well, okay then! I really had to think about that concept! They were happier than I was, at least on the surface.

At first, my tendency was to write off these women as not particularly bright. But the more I thought about it, the more I wondered who really was not very bright! Was it these women, who had accepted their place in the universe and seemed content? Or was it I, who could never find any real resolution to the problem and could not rest until I did? I found that, as much as I tried, I could not take that "leap of faith" that others seemed to have so little trouble doing.

At some point, I saw a statement to the effect that **when the student is ready, the teacher will appear**. I don't remember now where I first stumbled onto this adage. Various New Age philosophers have used it for years, but I have seen it in some of the old teachings, perhaps from Buddhism. I have come to believe that this statement is indeed true.

There was a time in my life when I was interested in astrology and a local university professor offered a course in drawing up horoscopes and invited me to join. I was interested in painting in oils and a friend who owned a craft shop approached me about taking a class her shop was offering. When I needed to know more about therapeutic recreation for a mental health day hospital where I was working, the graduate program at the University of North Carolina–Chapel Hill opened its doors to me and created just the program I needed.

Through the years, I have had a number of "teachers" who appeared exactly when I was ready to use whatever knowledge they had to impart. At any moment, there may be quite a few people around us who could teach us a lot. However, if we are not ready, we will never even notice that they are near. I have often wondered just how many wonderful bits of knowledge could have been mine if only I had been ready and what kind of difference they might have made in my life!

But I do have a concept of what is going on with the universe and just what my place in the overall picture is likely to be. I really didn't come to my conclusions from any one source. I will have to say that I was influenced more by some "teachers" than by others, but no one source fitted me exactly. I was intrigued by mysticism, but I didn't have the discipline for rigid meditation. I was interested in some of the concepts of Dianetics, but I found others to be stifling and just plain "off the wall" ridiculous. I found that psychological theories didn't go far enough and didn't explain everything I wanted to know. And I have already mentioned my problems with the "leap of faith" required by most organized religions. So, where did that leave me?

Frankly, it made me re-evaluate my own beliefs and forced me to develop my own theories about the universe and our reasons for being that bring me a semblance of comfort in this sometimes baffling world. That necessity has been a good thing for me. Actually, I have found some amazing "truths" and some very good ways to deal with the unknowns and the problems of the world. I gleaned a bit from every "teacher" or discipline I wandered into over the years. This book is organized by chapters on various subjects and included are mostly personal stories of how these concepts have come into my life and helped, in many cases, to make my life easier. At the very least, they have brought wonderment and "real magic" back into my life. I hope they will do the same for you.

So, open your mind and take off on your own fantastic voyage through the space-time continuum that is our universe!

3
A Tale of Synchronicity

The unthinkable had happened. I felt a terrible and deep sense of urgency, but the way was not clear. Everything around me was chaos. Smoke and dust clogged the air. I was having trouble breathing even though I was safe at the moment in my car. Also unclear was the reason, the catastrophe, and whether it was a natural disaster or the result of a manmade terrorist plot. I knew only that there was danger, imminent and terrifying, and that I had to act to save both myself and others. What, exactly, I was supposed to do to help was something I only hoped would eventually become clear. So I drove in my car, seeing the destruction of buildings and dodging piles of debris that almost blocked the road at times.

I drove and drove and I stopped when I finally saw other cars gathering at a big brick building that seemed to still be structurally sound. Parking hastily, I entered the building in search of others who would be allies in my quest, whatever that was.

For a few minutes, I wandered rather aimlessly through the halls. I could hear voices so I knew I was not alone. I kept walking toward the faint voices that grew louder as I got closer to the central part of the big building.

I first found a family—husband, wife, and two children. They were concerned and increasingly frantic, but didn't know what to do. The woman had two brothers she couldn't find and couldn't contact by phone. She was very worried.

I hurried down the hall, looking for others, and found another man who was also seeking people to join with in order to help. I learned he was an author and, strangely, he gave me a copy of his book. He was giving out copies to anyone he saw because it was a book on preparedness and survival during disasters, both manmade and natural. In the course of our conversation, he mentioned that his neighbor in a nearby town, that very morning, had stopped by his house and given him information about where he was going with his family so they would be safe. And, almost unbelievably, the neighbor who stopped by just happened to be one of the brothers of the lady with whom I had just talked. So I grabbed the man's arm and dragged him back down the hall so he could tell the sister where her brother was.

Then I continued on my quest, this time meeting a group of women who were making blankets and garments for any survivors of the disaster. There were stacks of blankets that they had hastily put together. I was amazed that they had done so much in the short time since the disaster struck. But they were at a standstill. They had run out of thread and couldn't find any in the town. I promised them I would ask around about thread and moved on down another hallway.

After meeting a few more people, I chanced to meet a man who gave me a brochure on survival techniques and, wonder of wonders, wrapped up in that brochure was a packet of thread and instructions about how to use it in various ways. When I inquired about the thread and told him about the group making blankets, he took me to his car that was filled with spools of thread. He owned a thread factory and he had an almost endless supply that was accessible. I hooked him up with the sewing group.

I walked farther down the hall and found another group who had fixed up one of the larger rooms to be a hospital of sorts, except that they had not managed to find a doctor. One man had nurse's training and he was trying to deal with several rather severe injuries. As I watched, several more people with injuries were helped into the area. As I continued on my way, in the next hall over, I came upon a woman who was bandaging a man's injured arm. When I inquired, she told me she was a doctor, so I sent her back to the makeshift hospital. She seemed grateful to have a direction and she led the injured man off in the direction of the hospital.

I found myself back close to the main entrance and I decided to check out other areas of town to see where I could help.

I went out to get into my car and found my car blocked by another car that had pulled up behind mine. The driver was still sitting in his car so I went to his open window to speak with him. When I asked him if he would move his car, I found he was a very friendly and helpful soul. We talked for a few minutes about the catastrophe (he didn't know what had caused it either), and I learned that he was the second missing brother of the first lady I had met, so I sent him to find his sister after he had moved his car.

Wow! So many coincidences! What were the chances? You might say, you just can't make this stuff up, but you would be wrong because I haven't told you one very important element of my story. This was all a dream I had several years ago! And it was odd in the way dreams often are, but it was a tale of **unconnected coincidences** or **synchronicity**.

If all these coincidences had happened in real life, we would have marveled over the strangeness of life and the odd curves it tends to throw us occasionally. In dreams, anything can and does happen. Nothing is beyond the realm of the imagination. Our minds can and do create incredible events, pictures, and happenings that boggle the mind and stretch our limits. But is this magic limited to our imagination and our dreams?

4
What is Synchronicity Anyway?

Just what is synchronicity? And is it real? Perhaps a bit of history on the derivation of the word would help.

Synchronicity is a word coined in the 1950s by psychiatrist and psychoanalyst, Dr. Carl Jung. It means a simultaneous occurrence of events that appear significantly related, but between which no discernable causal connection can be found. It is easy to dismiss such things in dreams, but when they happen in real life, they cause us to pause and ponder.

These events are "meaningful" coincidences. One writer described them as "cosmic assurances" to help us know we are on the right path in life. Others, especially those in various scientific fields, deny there is anything operating here other than really incredible coincidences.

Jung felt these odd occurrences were similar to dreams and that they provide messages in much the same manner. Some authors go even farther and hint that these "small miracles" link us to the universe at large and make us feel more closely connected to reasons for existence and reassure us that we have a place in the universe that is meaningful.

I have had a life filled with these incidents. I have also come to realize that there are no such things as "meaningless coincidences" and I believe nothing happens without a reason.

Some of my incidents of synchronicity are very involved and complex. The odds of these events happening as they did are truly astronomical. I remember that someone described synchronistic events happening by chance as having odds so great that they

What is Synchronicity Anyway?

would not happen even in the billions of years left in the remainder of the expected lifetime of the universe! Those are pretty big odds!

You have all had small examples of synchronicity, I'm sure, in your everyday life. You try to think of someone's name and that person either calls you or you see his name somewhere. You think about calling a friend and he or she calls you. You can't think of a word and the word appears an hour or so later in the book you are reading. We tend to overlook these subtle coincidences all the time. I think the universe is answering us with these events. All you need to do is listen. You will find examples of synchronicity happening much more often when you are aware of them.

Several days ago, I was walking on my road near my home with my daughter. We were talking about a pair of twins who grew up near us and we were wondering about some circumstances surrounding their early childhood. Almost immediately, a car pulled off the road beside us and the driver was the grandfather of the twins we were discussing. In the course of our conversation with the grandfather, he just happened to mention the circumstances we were talking about and he told us just what happened. We didn't even ask!

Have you ever lost something and then dreamed where to find the lost object? I have. I lost a sentimental necklace several years ago and I spent weeks looking for it. Then, one night, I dreamed the necklace was caught on the back of a rack in my pantry. Thankfully, I remembered the dream when I awoke. I kind of laughed to think that I was actually going to go look where my dream told me to look. Then I looked. There, caught on the back side of a rack in my pantry dangled my necklace! I have no idea how it got there or when it happened. But there it was. I cannot explain how I could find the answer in my dream, but I did. All I can say is God works in mysterious ways and I wonder if we will ever really understand. I think there are some things we just have to accept. (I guess that acceptance is *my* leap of faith!)

5

The Bandleader's Vision

In the '60s and '70s, a popular Charlotte bandleader named Jerry Goodman led a number of bands, including *The Jerry Goodman Group* and *The Gootmon Saurkraut Show Band*, which were very popular at country club and private party events all over the East Coast. Both of these bands occasionally played in the mountains of western North Carolina at the area ski resorts.

On a summer weekend in the late '60s, *The Jerry Goodman Group* was booked in the North Carolina High Country and the band was given accommodations in a very nice chalet near the resort. The band played to a packed house on Friday evening and was booked to play again on Saturday night.

The band members, tired from the travel from Charlotte, the couple of hours of setting up all the equipment, and then playing for the four-hour dance, went to bed exhausted and planned to sleep late and have a leisurely day until time to play again.

The bandleader, Jerry Goodman, woke up early the next morning. He lay there for a while and then decided he wouldn't be able to go back to sleep and might as well get up. Everyone else was still asleep and showed no signs of movement. A cup of coffee would be good, he thought, so he got dressed and quietly let himself out of the chalet. Outside, he realized he would have to drive somewhere in order to find breakfast, or even that cup of coffee, so he got in his van and took off on his search.

In the small town at the foot of the mountain, he found some open shops and a couple of restaurants. He grabbed a breakfast sandwich and that welcome cup of coffee and decided to explore the area on his own before the band members woke up.

He drove through the small town and headed toward the road that linked several small High Country towns. He drove for some distance on several of the back roads and briefly considered going to one of the High Country attractions such as Grandfather Mountain and the Mile-High Swinging Bridge, but decided he didn't have the time. So he kept going for a few miles, enjoying the sunshine and the pretty day.

At some point, Jerry ended up near another of the area's small towns and, looking across a meadow from the main road, he saw a rock house nestled against a mountain. The house looked as if it had grown there naturally, rather than having been built. It nestled under the curve of the mountain behind it and the granite blended into the mountainside. Roses in full bloom climbed up both sides of the entryway and also covered one of the side walls. A full hemlock hedge ran around three sides of the yard. Majestic old pines surrounded the back of the house and graced both sides.

He was enchanted by the sight and pulled off for a closer look. He had the passing thought that he would like to meet the people who lived in that house and would like to see the inside. He also decided the owners of the house might not take kindly to someone knocking on their door just to tell them how much he liked their house and, since he had a tight schedule that day, he returned to the resort to get ready for his job.

In the years that followed, Jerry tried to ride by the enchanting house when he was in the area and had some free time. He never stopped, however.

Jerry Goodman was my neighbor when I moved into an apartment complex in Charlotte. I knew he was a bandleader because he had a 5x8 trailer that was often hooked up to his van that proclaimed: *The Jerry Goodman Group*. But I would have known even if I had not seen the trailer. He had band practice in his apartment! And he was my next-door neighbor. Actually, he had the end apartment, so there was no one to disturb on the other side of him. When trumpet notes lasted until after midnight, I threw books against the wall. When that did no good, I wrote letters of complaint to the management. They told me there had to be letters of complaint from two different residents before something could be done. Two residents? I was his only neighbor.

So I went to see him to complain in person after a particularly loud band session. He was shocked. He thought the apartments were quite soundproof because, as he said, "I never heard a peep out of you!" But he did try to be a little quieter after that and to hold band practices that didn't run into the wee hours.

His sister and her family lived in the apartment across the street. She was a dancer/dance instructor and her husband was a records promoter. They always had an interesting parade of people visiting. My kitchen window looked out on their doorway and I watched the antics in amusement! Once, I saw Jerry running over to their place with a frying pan full of scrambled eggs!

But Jerry was always friendly when I saw him. On two occasions, he rang the doorbell to borrow a cup of sugar or milk when I was in the shower. By the second time, I accused him of listening until he heard my shower running before he came to borrow something! He just grinned. But then he started asking me to go to some of the dances where his band played. I was fascinated with what he could do with keyboards!

Jerry had come out fourth in the world on accordion when he was nineteen in international competition. He was offered a spot on Lawrence Welk, but he decided to go on tour with *The Three Suns* instead. (Otherwise, it might have been Jerry Goodman instead of Myron Floren who played the accordion all those years with Lawrence Welk!)

We dated for some months, and then got engaged. I decided it was time to take Jerry to meet my parents who lived in the mountains of western North Carolina where I had grown up.

The Bandleader's Vision

On the winding road up the mountain, Jerry started telling me about his many trips to the North Carolina High Country and he finally talked about the house he had seen many years earlier. He thought maybe I would know who lived there. I agreed that I might and, if he would point out the house, I would see if I could answer his question.

As we came around a big curve in a tiny hamlet at the top of the long mountain ridge, Jerry grew excited.

"That house is really close here, I think," he said. "Maybe you really will know who lives there."

We pulled into my parents' driveway and Jerry sat in shock, staring at the rock house, covered in roses, surrounded by the high hemlock hedge, and nestled under the side of the mountain.

He shook his head in disbelief. "You won't believe this. This is the house I have wondered about for years. Your parents *really* live here?"

In the next few minutes, he not only got to go inside the house that had fascinated him for years, but he also got to meet the people who lived there! What an incredible coincidence! Or not!

Through the years, Jerry and I marveled at such an amazing coincidence. The chances of those events happening must be astronomical, at least. For the person who grew up in that house to move in next door to the person who wanted to meet the people who lived in that house in a city one hundred miles from the North Carolina mountains boggles the mind, doesn't it?

How are such things possible? The distance, both in space and in time, between these apparently unconnected events makes one have a hard time believing everything was just chance, doesn't it? All these years later, I am still baffled and astonished by the "coincidence."

I am also a firm believer in the adage, "Your thoughts create your future." Jerry's passing thought on that day years ago certainly set in motion a series of events that culminated in his getting his wish. Considering everything, another old adage probably should be mentioned—"Be careful what you wish for; you just might get it."

6

Oktoberfest Phenomenon

My daughter and I met Ed and Nan at a local resort where dances are held once a week every summer. We liked them a lot. They were the kind of people who end up in charge of everything. Ed manned the door, checking the registrations against the people who actually came to make sure we were all accounted for. Nan brought food and generally looked out for everyone.

My daughter and Nan hit it off even though Nan was around my age. They made plans to get together and they visited every time there was a dance at the resort.

We spent all summer talking with each other when we were at the dances and liked each other better every time we met. We learned things about each other. However, we obviously didn't learn everything and we soon found that out in a rather unusual way.

One early fall night, we all found ourselves at an outdoor music venue, listening to live entertainment and enjoying the crisp autumn air in the mountains. The band played *Rocky Top* and several people got up and started clogging.

Ed was sitting beside me and he remarked, "I used to clog. In fact, I found my old clogging shoes the other day. I had worn them just about out!"

"That's funny," I said. "I never wore out shoes clogging, but I did wear out several pairs of shoes doing the polka with *The Gootmon Sauerkraut Band*!"

"What band did you say?" he asked.

The MAGIC Within

"The Gootmon Sauerkraut Band."

Ed looked at me in puzzlement and finally said, "I've known *The Gootmon Sauerkraut Band* for fifty years! I've known Jerry Goodman for fifty years! Well, maybe not quite that long, but I booked *The Gootmon Sauerkraut Band* at Castle McCulloch in Jamestown near Greensboro for five years straight for the Castle McCulloch Oktoberfest!"

"Ed, *I* booked the Castle McCulloch Oktoberfest for *The Gootmon Sauerkraut Band* for five years in a row! You had to have booked it with *me*. I handled all the booking for Jerry's bands during that time," I said, shaking my head in wonder over the coincidence.

"I just can't believe it. What a small world it is!"

I pulled out my phone and called Jerry in Charlotte and he and Ed spent a few minutes reconnecting after all the years that had passed. We told each other we would go to Charlotte one evening and have dinner at the restaurant where Jerry occasionally plays German music on his accordion.

We spent the rest of the evening reminiscing over our shared connection from the distant past.

When I got home that night, I kept thinking about the unusual connection and the coincidence of finding out that I had known our new good friends thirty years ago in another life! And then I remembered that I had taken videos occasionally during the years that I was dancing with the German band. So I pulled out my old videos that my daughter had transferred to DVD.

There was a disc entitled "Castle McCulloch" and I pulled it out and put it in the player. Imagine my shock when a tall, good-looking guy in lederhosen and a Bavarian hat strode across the stage, grabbed the microphone, and announced, "Hi! I'm Ed and I'm the *burgermeister* of Castle McCulloch. Welcome to Oktoberfest at

Oktoberfest Phenomenon

Castle McCulloch."

Yes, it was my new/old friend Ed minus about thirty years! But it definitely was him. I had set up a video camera at the side of the stage and just let it run for the performances. I was excited about showing the video to Ed and Nan.

But then, I let the video play on to see what else I had captured while we were playing for the Castle McCulloch Oktoberfest. Wait, there was MUCH more!

Suddenly I danced on stage with Ed as my partner doing the polka! We danced and danced around the stage.

This video was really funny because Ed's lederhosen straps chose that time to fall off his shoulders. He kept pushing them back up again and again, to no avail. Finally, he just shrugged out of the straps entirely and let them flop around while we continued to polka!

And there, as the video played on, was "The Littlest Gootmon," my daughter dancing at the side of the stage in her red and white dirndl!

In fact, I sent the clip of Ed and me dancing to Ed and Nan and they got a big laugh from it. But none of us could believe the past connection. The connection we never would have been aware of except for the chance mention of wearing out clogging shoes and polka shoes!

There was a little more synchronicity. The Sugar Mountain Oktoberfest was scheduled to take place on that weekend. Ed suggested that we all attend the Oktoberfest and re-create our polka dancing from all those years ago. When we figured it up, we found that our polka dancing at Castle McCulloch took place twenty-nine years to the day before the Sugar Mountain Oktoberfest! And we did go re-create our dance. I even managed to fit in the same dirndl I wore in the old video! Ed and I danced the polka while my daughter and Nan videotaped our re-creation. What a great gift from the past!

7

Psychic Synchronicity

Years ago for a time, I lived in the North Carolina city of Charlotte. One day, after I had been in the city for several months, I heard a local psychic interviewed on the radio. This lady's name was Pat Gabriel. I don't recall that she did more than briefly discuss her abilities. She didn't make any predictions, but she was interesting enough that, when she gave out her phone number, I wrote it down.

A few days later, I called and made an appointment for my very own reading with this supposed psychic. I had never had a psychic reading before, so I really didn't know what to expect.

She lived in a nice apartment in an upper middle-class neighborhood. I don't know what I expected as far as her appearance was concerned, either, but she was small, a tiny bit plump, attractive, and reminded me of singers Brenda Lee or Leslie Gore with her blond upsweep and careful makeup.

She was very friendly and I was immediately at ease in her presence. She ushered me into a room with a table holding a deck of cards.

The first thing Pat asked me was if she could hold my watch for a minute. I gave it to her and she held it and shut her eyes.

"You are from the North Carolina mountains, and you have been dabbling in pastels for the past three weeks," she told me.

I was stunned. It was true. I had come to Charlotte from the mountains and I also had been drawing pictures with pastels for the previous three weeks. How could she know that? We had had absolutely no conversations of any personal nature. We made the appointment and said no more. When I arrived we introduced ourselves, she showed me into the room, and there was no further conversation except her asking me for my watch. Boy!

In the ensuing reading, she told me I would be going to a retreat in the mountains near Asheville and I would meet this man that I would date for a while. He would look a lot like Alex Trebek of *Jeopardy*. Then she told me I would have a child, a little girl, who would have blond hair, blue or green eyes, and would be a Virgo or a Leo and that she would lead me on a merry chase!

I was very curious and I asked her how she was able to know these things. She said she felt her abilities came from God and He helped her help others. She showed me a check she had written to herself for the amount she wanted to earn for the year and she signed it "From God."

I don't remember much else, but I went home happy because I was in my early 30s and I had given up on meeting that special someone again and having a child. I had been divorced for several years and my relationships since then had not worked out for one reason or another.

A couple of months later, I had the occasion to attend a weeklong mental health seminar at Mount Pisgah near Asheville and, sure enough, I met and started dating a man from Raleigh who looked a lot like Alex Trebek!

I was charmed by Pat and I saw her again once or twice in the next year or so. The man from Raleigh finally disappeared. A long-distance romance was hard to maintain.

Eventually, a local bandleader, Jerry Goodman, moved into the apartment beside mine. We started dating and ultimately got engaged. One day, I mentioned Pat's name to Jerry and he surprised me by telling me he had dated Pat Gabriel for a while.

"In fact," he said, "why don't we go out to lunch with her. I haven't seen her in a long time. I'll call her."

He called Pat and they made arrangements for us to meet for lunch a couple of days later. I was amazed that my fiancé had a close connection to the lady who had given me a couple of psychic readings and in as big a city as Charlotte. It was quite another example of synchronicity. What were the odds?

Pat was already seated when we got to the restaurant. As we walked in, Pat's eyes widened, she paled visibly, and her mouth opened in surprise.

"Nancy," she said, "do you remember about the child I told you that you would have? Well, Jerry will be the father. She just walked in with you!"

The rest of the story is that Jerry and I did have that blond-haired, green-eyed child who is a Virgo just exactly as Pat predicted. And interestingly, she and Pat formed a close friendship and talked often through the years until Pat's passing. My daughter has missed her advice very much in the years since.

I don't profess to even begin to understand how some people in our present-day world seem to be able to peer into the future. But it appears they can!

8

Synchronicity on the Cascade Loop

It was going to be a wonderful trip to California. My very good friend Marilyn and I were going to fly into Sacramento, rent a car, and drive up the Pacific Coast, visiting with one of our school friends on the way.

About the same time as we were planning our trip, we learned that another of our friends, Phyllis, had been talking with a guy from Seattle on a dating site for six months or so and she was planning to go to Seattle to meet him about the same time we were going to be on the West Coast. She had not actually met the guy she was going to see. She realized that she might get to Seattle and not actually like this guy or trust him. We told her that we would be driving up from Sacramento to Seattle and would be in the general area for about two weeks, so that if she found herself in an awkward situation, we could just pick her up and she could go on the rest of our trip with us. I think she was very grateful to have such a convenient "out," and surprised (as we were) that our time on the West Coast dovetailed so well. So, a few days later, Phyllis left on a flight to Seattle and Marilyn and I took our plane to Sacramento.

Marilyn and I visited with our friends near Oroville for several days and then said our goodbyes and departed for our leisurely drive up the coast. Marilyn talked with Phyllis who assured her that she was having a great time and didn't need to be picked up. We breathed a sigh of relief and headed north.

We had a wonderful trip up the California coast, stopping whenever we saw anything that interested us and spending the night when we were tired of driving. We took pictures of elk herds and redwood forests and windswept beaches and, in general, had a great time.

Synchronicity on the Cascade Loop

After California, we drove on up the Oregon coast. We were amazed to see the tsunami warning signs all along the coastal route. At one point at Gold Beach, we stopped and spent the day on a wild boat ride up the Rogue River. The cowboy driving our boat kept doing wheelies in the eddies and small waterfalls and that got a bit rough on my back, but it was great fun and we had a ball.

Marilyn had family in Washington State in the town of Rockport and she wanted to visit with them. Her father had spent many years there and these people were his friends and relatives. So we made our way to Rockport.

We spent a night with Marilyn's relatives and got some great tips on what not to miss as we explored areas of Washington State in the days ahead. Marilyn wanted to explore the Cascade Loop, a 400-mile circle through the Cascade Mountains. I didn't know much about the Loop, but it sounded like a wonderful trip.

We started out early and found ourselves without a cell phone signal for much of the morning. It was a beautiful drive, through some of the most picturesque scenery, rivaling even our own mountains of North Carolina.

We stopped for a while at Ross Lake near Diablo Dam and took pictures of each other and the crystal blue lake. The water looked like the water of the Caribbean. We reluctantly got back on the road and soon came around a curve just seconds after a landslide blocked the right lane. Marilyn was driving (my back was still sore from the boat ride!) and she managed to dodge the debris in the road. Thank goodness there was no one coming!

A little while later, we heard pings from our cell phones. We finally had service after several hours of being without any way to communicate. Marilyn had another ping signaling that she had a message and she put the phone to her ear to listen. (Of course, at that time, it was not illegal to listen to or send messages yet!)

She was driving and I was navigating and I was looking at our map to see what was close while she listened to her message.

"Nancy, can you see where Winthrop is?" she asked me.

I started to check my map, but just before I bent my head, I saw a road sign that said, "Winthrop one mile."

I read the road sign to Marilyn, who started laughing.

"You are not going to believe this," she said. "Phyllis and her new friend are eating lunch at a sidewalk café in Winthrop right now! Let's go join them for lunch! They won't believe it, either!"

Well, we drove on in to the little town and, sure enough, there were Phyllis and Steve sitting at a sidewalk café having lunch. Boy, it blew their minds when we pulled up and got out of our car, waving at them!

After we got over being almost dumbfounded at the synchronicity, we tried to figure out how we had all come together in the same location at this point in time.

Marilyn and I had started out on the 400-mile Cascade Loop from the (roughly) southwest end and had headed northeast on the Loop. We had not talked with Phyllis since finding out she was okay. We thought she was still back in Seattle. Phyllis had no idea where we were, either, and certainly didn't know we were exploring the Cascade Loop.

Phyllis and Steve had come into the Loop from the southeast and had gone up the eastern side. They had spent the night in the little German town of Leavenworth and had driven on around to Winthrop that morning. They were heading to Ross Lake and Diablo Dam and were traveling on the same way from which we had just come.

And, of course, it made perfect sense to find out where Phyllis and Steve had stayed in Leavenworth and to make that our target motel for the night! Coincidence, coincidence, coincidence!

So, Marilyn and I got to meet Phyllis' new friend before anyone else in North Carolina did. Steve and Phyllis eventually got engaged and he made the move to North Carolina.

There were several things that had to happen in order for this example of synchronicity to take place.

• The cell phone service had to come back on exactly when it did, otherwise we would have missed Phyllis' message and would have driven right through Winthrop without checking to see who was dining at the sidewalk café.

• Phyllis had to send her message to us just exactly when she did. Any earlier and we would have had no service. Any later and we would have left Winthrop far behind us and we probably wouldn't have turned around.

• Phyllis and Steve had to pick that particular time to stop for lunch.

• Marilyn and I had to leave Ross Lake exactly when we did for us to be in the vicinity of Winthrop when we got Phyllis' message.

None of us realized we were within hundreds of miles of each other. We had planned to catch up with Phyllis later in the week when we returned to Seattle to catch our flight home to North Carolina. Synchronicity, serendipity, or the hand of God—call it what you will—the whole scenario was very strange! (And much too strange for chance!)

9

Synchronicity at the Falls

A few years ago, Bruce and I hiked to Linville Falls on the trail from the Wiseman's View road in western North Carolina. We had a pleasant walk and met a lovely family from Southern Pines. The father was a runner. Bruce, a runner himself and owner and founder of *Running Journal*, spotted him immediately! We had a nice chat with the family and discovered that the father and Bruce knew some of the same people. Anyway, we had a nice conversation, visited for a few minutes, wished each other well, and went on our way. The family headed on to another overlook and Bruce and I headed back to the gravel parking lot. When we reached our car, we decided to go grab lunch at a nearby restaurant in the area. It was an hour or so before we got back on the road and continued our sightseeing trip.

We stopped at a couple of scenic overlooks. Then I decided to show Bruce the good fishing and picnicking spots off the Blue Ridge Parkway. So, of course, we visited the Linville Falls picnic area and drove all around there. Then, totally on a whim, I had him drive across the Blue Ridge Parkway to the camping area on the other side. I had camped in that campground several times over the years, but I had not been there for a long time and I wanted to see it again.

At the end of a fairly long road into the campground, we again met up with the family from Southern Pines. I didn't think much about it, figuring that they had originally gone in to the Falls from this side and were parked in the paved campground lot. But when we headed back out the way we came, we saw the family walking along the road back to the Parkway. I knew they either wanted to take a very long walk or were lost. It turns out they were lost. They had mistakenly taken the branch of the trail that leads to the Parkway parking lot instead of the one to the gravel lot off the Wiseman's View road. So, we drove the grateful family several miles back to their car.

I have a firm belief that there are no coincidences and that everything happens for a reason. Things are consistently happening to me that reinforce my belief.

Obviously, if we had not made the acquaintance of the family earlier in the day at the Falls, we would not have noticed or thought it strange that several people were walking beside the road. And we would not have stopped to check on them. Odd how things just come together when they need to, isn't it?

10

Synchronicity in a Small World

It started innocently enough at my newspaper office. It was an ordinary day, not close enough to deadline day to worry or be in a great hurry. I was turning through the newly arrived faxes and found an obituary for my neighbor, Dot. I had been in out of town for several days and I didn't know she had died. Then I opened my new e-mails for the newspaper and found an obituary for Jim, an Avery County native who had been my athletic coach at St. Andrews University in the sixties.

I mentioned to our newly hired writer, Becky Alghrary, that it was strange to learn of the deaths of both my neighbor and my old coach at St. Andrews in this manner. Becky had the office next to mine and, as we could hear each other plainly, we often talked around our mutual wall!

Becky immediately asked when I was at St. Andrews. I told her I graduated in 1966. She said two of her old boyfriends had attended St. Andrews in the sixties and asked if I had known either Ray Gilchrist or Roy Wilson.

Stunned, I told her I had known Ray and I had married Roy three weeks after I graduated from St. Andrews.

Becky, who was as stunned as I was, said she had dated Roy during the two years they were together at Lees-McRae College. She went on to say that Roy had broken her heart when he transferred to St. Andrews and started dating a girl named Nancy that she heard he later married.

None of her conversation made sense at first. Then it did!

Synchronicity in a Small World

"Oh my gosh!" I gasped. "You're Becky Ikard!" (I had never known Becky Alghrary's maiden name.)

I well remembered Becky Ikard. In the fall of my sophomore year at St. Andrews, I started dating Roy, who was a wonderful man (and still is) from Charlotte. Roy and I had gone out for several weeks and the relationship appeared to have possibilities. We both decided to pursue it and see where it led. At that point in time, Roy had already made plans to go home the next weekend to see a girl he had been dating named Becky Ikard. I remember he agonized about telling her he was now dating me. However, Fall Fling at St. Andrews was that weekend and I really wanted to go. Roy finally called Becky and told her he was dating someone else and cancelled his date with her. So, we went to Fall Fling together.

In truth, I never thought too much more about Becky Ikard. I did see a picture he had in his wallet of this blond girl and she was really cute. I also will admit that, in all the intervening years, every time I went by the I-40 exit to the town of Icard, I had a momentary thought about Becky Ikard.

A chance remark changed everything. We had known each other for years. But if I had not mentioned St. Andrews, Becky and I would have worked together right on and never would have known our pasts were intertwined. But that is not the end of the story. Becky and I have more incidents of synchronicity.

It turns out that we both attended the visitation in Charlotte when Roy's father died. (Of course, Roy didn't introduce his ex-wife and his ex-girlfriend!)

Several years ago when I was hired to be the general manager of the *Avery Mountain Times*, Becky and I both applied for the job. Owner Ken Ketchie told Becky that he was hiring me because I was from the county and knew everybody there. I never knew Becky had applied. I didn't know her well at that time.

When I married Bruce and was looking for someone to take my place at the *Mountain Times*, I tried to hire Becky. A local lawyer had just offered her a job and she decided to take it.

Over the months I was the publisher of *The Avery Journal-Times*, I ran into Becky several times and always encouraged her to consider writing for my newspaper. When I came back to the newspaper for the second time, our first new hire was Becky and I was delighted.

My mention of St. Andrews University to Becky sent me on one of those rare, special twists that life sometimes grants us. Like I said, there are no accidents and it really is a small, small world after all!

11

Inspirational Synchronicity

In 2017, I was looking through my back text messages and I found one dated 2014 that, for some unknown reason, I had never seen before. It read:

I just wanted to thank you for your beautiful artwork!

My name is Sandra Curtis and I live in Cincinnati, Ohio. I am the single mother of three wonderful young adult children that I could not be prouder of! Times were not always easy, but we managed to do all right and two of the three are college graduates and the other is a professional athlete. I always told my children that sometimes you have to sacrifice for the good of the family and that dreams might be delayed, but never denied!

While my oldest son was in school, he always told me he would one day be able to give me things that I sacrificed so they all could pursue their dreams. He moved to Cary, NC, in November of 2012, about five months after he graduated from pharmacy school.

In April, 2014, I was able to visit him for the first time. It was a wonderful trip full of firsts for me. I had never been to the ocean and he and his girlfriend took me to Wilmington, NC. I cried at the magnificence of the ocean's beauty and majesty.

My son was so proud of himself for granting me the opportunity to experience something so wonderful and grand as well as orchestrating my first vacation in over 20 years!

While in Wilmington, we visited Crescent Moon Art Gallery and I fell in love with your painting "Colorful Reflections." I felt a strong sense of peace and joy immediately upon seeing it. I knew it would probably be damaged if I took it home with me on the airplane so my plan was to go home and have it shipped possibly. I was hesitant because of habits of many years, which required that I only buy necessities. I took the owner's card and wondered if I would ever be able to buy that beautiful piece of tranquility.

I was about to leave the store when the owner asked me to go look at some other works I might be interested in. Not being in love with anything in the shop more than your painting, I left the store a bit saddened.

The day before I was to return to Cincinnati, we all went out for a wonderful dinner and fun. When we returned to my son's apartment, he popped the trunk of his car and his girlfriend asked me to help her get something out of the trunk. It was your painting, "Colorful Reflections"!!!!

They had purchased the painting while the shop owner was showing me the other works. They mailed the picture to me in Cincinnati and I have the pleasure of looking at it every day of my life!

It hangs over my desk that I run my small business from and am writing my dissertation on. I cannot tell you how much inspiration and peace it provides me, and the smile on my son's and his girlfriend's faces when they showed me the painting was absolutely priceless! My son said the cost of the picture was nothing compared to the look on my face when they gave it to me.

Thank you for giving me peace, inspiration, and the strength to actually start living life, and not just existing or enduring!

I cried. I was so humbled and pleased that someone had found my painting so inspirational. I immediately texted Sandra and told her I had just received her message. Who knows where it had been for three years? I'm so glad it finally showed up and I didn't miss it.

During the next few days, we had a long visit on the phone. I found out she had first seen the ocean on Wrightsville Beach very near Wilmington.

Oddly, I had recently completed a painting of the ocean, the beach, and dunes fencing at one of the beach entrances at Wrightsville.

Inspirational Synchronicity

I had taken a photograph of that scene a couple of years before, intending to do a painting of it when I had time. That photograph stayed on my computer desktop and I was reminded that I should paint it for months. I finally did and it turned out really well. I could almost feel the sand on my feet!

Because Sandra had loved my "Colorful Reflections" painting and she had seen the ocean for the first time, I thought she might like the "Wrightsville Dunes" painting so I sent her a print of the painting.

Imagine my surprise when she sent me a text with a picture of her at the Wrightsville Beach entrance where she saw the ocean for the first time and it was the same entrance with the same fencing that I had painted and of which I had sent her the print! What were the odds?

12

Synchronicity from My Childhood

A good friend of mine who lived near the Hilton Head and Edisto Beach area decided to fix me up with a friend of the man she was currently dating. The only thing was, I lived in the mountains of western North Carolina and he lived on an island off the coast of South Carolina. There was quite a distance between our locations. His name was Bill and he came all the way to the mountains with his RV to meet me, parked in a campground for the night, and then he took me out to dinner. We had a pleasant evening and enjoyed getting to know each other. He told me about his family. He had a son and a daughter and a couple of young adult grandchildren.

He left early the next morning and he called several times over the course of a couple of weeks. Finally, he called and said his family was coming to the island for Thanksgiving and asked if my daughter and I would like to come down also. We decided going to the South Carolina coast might be a fun way to spend the holiday. So we did.

Bill's wife had died years earlier. His son lived in the area and the grandsons, who were in high school, spent as much time at their grandfather's place as they did at their own home. His daughter lived in Greenville, SC, and she and her boyfriend were coming for the holiday also. She was close to my age as Bill was 15 or so years older than I was. I was looking forward to meeting them all.

My daughter and I made a leisurely trip to the coast and got there in the late afternoon. Bill's house actually was on an island and was absolutely gorgeous. The whole island was! That was a nice way of life for anyone who wanted to avoid the stress and strain of today's busy world.

Synchronicity from My Childhood

The daughter, Emily, and her boyfriend Ed got there just after we did. Emily was easygoing and I found she was fun to be around. Ed was a roly-poly guy who seemed content enough to stay in the background while Emily joked and told funny stories.

The weekend passed in a flurry of great meals and short trips around the area. We met the son and all the grandchildren and went to see Bill's place of business.

On Saturday, we had enjoyed a large meal and were sitting around the living room relaxing, dreading our travels back home to colder weather the next day.

We were talking about how much we loved the mountains. I can't remember just how it came about, but at some point Ed remarked that he really enjoyed the North Carolina mountains. In fact, he said, he had spent some of the happiest years of his youth attending a summer camp in the NC mountains.

We talked for a while about camps and how the camps when Ed and I were growing up aren't really around much anymore. They were private and children usually attended them for most of the summer. Now there is more daycare in the summer and other activities so parents keep their children home and use day programs. I talked about how I thought my years at summer camps were a very important part of my life. I learned horseback riding and participated in horseshows, learned tennis, drama, swimming and got my junior lifesaving certificate, art, writing, and many more fun things that many kids today miss.

Ed said his summer camp experience was equally as important, although the camp he attended operated for only two years and he didn't go after that.

"Where was your camp located," I asked him.

"It was near Hendersonville, but you probably never heard of it since it was in existence for only those two years."

At this point, I was getting goose bumps because somehow I knew what he was going to say.

"Try me," I said.

"It was Camp Glen-Barry," he said. "It was run by the president of—"

"Coker College from Hartsville, SC. Dr. and Mrs. Barry ran the camp for two years!" I finished the sentence for him.

We stared at each in complete shock.

"Who are you? What is your last name?" I asked.

"Stone, but I wasn't called Ed back then. Everybody called me Butch."

"Oh my goodness, Butch Stone! I knew you well! I was Nancy Stroupe and Odes was my brother! You were cabin mates and his best friend at camp! And Jean? What happened to your sister Jean?"

"Nancy! Boy, it is a small world, isn't it? Jean is good. She lives not too far from me. She will be so surprised! I'll give you her contact info."

I had spent eight weeks the two summers I was fourteen and fifteen at Camp Glen-Barry in Hendersonville. I had attended several different summer camps both before and after my time at Glen-Barry, but Glen-Barry was always my favorite and was the one where I made the most friends, some who were still friends of mine years later.

Butch actually did put me in touch with his sister Jean and we caught up. But I didn't go back down to the island again. I concluded that the lifestyle and the partying hard just wasn't something I wanted to embrace for my future. So, it was a very good thing that Butch and I chanced to mention the mountains and thereby discovered our shared childhood memories and time. If we had not had that conversation, we would have gone on our merry way not realizing we had spent time with a friend from our childhood! That feeling of synchronicity is just too strange and magical for words!

13

Myles Standish Revisited

When I was a child, the school library had some very interesting books that were biographies of famous people. These books were orange with black silhouettes of heads on the covers. If you are over fifty, you probably have seen these books. They were in every school library. One, in particular, stood out to me. It was the biography of Myles Standish.

I don't know why I was so taken with that book. I know I thought the name was very pretty. I read the book several times over the course of a couple of years and I always enjoyed it. Standish was a hero of sorts to me all through my early school years.

Imagine my surprise—and pleasure—several years ago when my husband pointed out a man while we were eating in a Greeneville restaurant and said, "That is the best carpenter you will ever find. His name is Myles Standish and, if you want to have anything done at the house, he is the person to do it."

I'll have to admit that I thought he was teasing me. "No way," I told him. I really didn't believe him, although why he would say the guy's name was Myles Standish, I didn't know. There was no way he could have known of my early fascination with Myles Standish.

Then the man in question came by our table and Bruce introduced me. I was shocked to learn that his name really was Myles Standish and that he was a direct descendent of the original Myles Standish. I learned from him that there has been a Myles in every generation since the original Myles.

The original Myles Standish was one of the 102 English settlers who came to America on the Mayflower in 1620. According to biographers, he was a professional soldier who was hired by the Pilgrims as a military advisor for the Plymouth Colony.

Standish was born in 1584 in England and grew up in a well-known and wealthy family. In his family, there was a conflict over religion, which started about the time Myles was born. Although Myles apparently was baptized Catholic, it is believed by many that he later became a Protestant. Apparently, he never joined a church in the New World. Many believe that his family's religious conflict was the reason.

Another mystery in Myles' life is why his family members did not allow him to receive his share of the family inheritance. At any rate, hurt and disillusioned, he left his family home and started his military career.

Standish was eventually hired by the Pilgrims to be their military captain. He was one of the group members who signed the Mayflower Compact at Cape Cod on November 11, 1620.

Standish died in Duxbury, Massachusetts, on October 3, 1656. He is remembered as being the Pilgrim Colony's representative in England and as an assistant to the governor and the colony's treasurer. He was also one of the founders of the town of Duxbury. He had a reputation for bravery in battle and led a force that saved a settlement under attack by Indians.

The biography I read as a child probably romanticized Myles Standish. Later biographies I have read describe him as being small in stature and rather ferocious in nature. However, his deeds were such that he always will be remembered as a hero.

I want to tell you a little about the present generation Myles Standish, who is in his own way every bit as much a hero.

After Bruce introduced us, I got Myles' number and, when I was ready to do some renovations to my house, I called Myles. As soon as he was free, Myles and I undertook some major renovations to the Greeneville house. (Actually, I planned and Myles figured out how to come up with what I wanted!) We spent a lot of time together in the couple of years he worked on the house and I grew to greatly appreciate and dearly love this gentle bear of a man.

Myles was a wonderful carpenter, but he was so much more than that. By this time, it did not surprise me to find out that he had a number of advanced degrees, one of which was in theology. He opted out of that field because one of his two daughters had died of leukemia and he was furious that God had let something so awful happen. He spent some years working in special education. At some point, he had become disillusioned by the red tape in our education system and had opted out of that field also. He felt like all the requirements and red tape hampered seriously his efforts to help special needs children. (Sounds a lot like the original Standish, doesn't it?) He chose to work with his hands and at his own pace in work situations of his own choosing. I think he was a much happier man because of his choices.

Some time later, Myles was diagnosed with a stage IV melanoma on his shoulder. He had surgery and then chemotherapy. He had a rough time of it, but he never lost his ability to smile or his concern for others. I thought, and hoped, he was okay.

Before long, he was back working at my house and at our rental house with the same cheerful demeanor he always had. I'm sure there were some bad days, but Myles never let on. He did tell me the chemo had kicked his butt and he decided not to finish the course, but he was doing some alternative treatments and he thought it would be all right.

We talked about every subject under the sun. We discussed philosophy, religion, child-rearing techniques, art, history, and Myles knew a lot about all of these things (and always had an opinion!).

He was so proud of his daughter, Julie, and her accomplishments and he always had wonderful things to say about his beloved Mary Ann, his significant other.

He left small kindnesses in his wake. When I would come home to Greeneville after a week spent in the High Country putting out the newspaper, there would be some sort of treat in the refrigerator with a note that read, "This is made with artificial sweetener so Nancy can eat it. Love, Myles." (This after I learned I was diabetic.)

After I had rotator cuff surgery and couldn't drive, Myles showed up in Bruce's office and told him he was sure I wanted to come to Greeneville for the weekend and he was going to go to the High Country to get me and then take me back on Monday—and he did! And while he was at the newspaper office, he totally charmed the whole staff. He told them all about the original Myles Standish. They loved him.

On the way back from Greeneville on Monday morning, Myles told me that he had been in the hospital with pneumonia for a few days several weeks before. I didn't realize that. I hadn't heard. He said he really thought he was going to die while he was in the hospital. He said he got a cold and in a day or so was so sick that he had to be taken to the hospital by ambulance. He said he was surprised that he recovered and got to come home. So, again, I thought all was well and I was so very glad.

A couple of weeks later, I was devastated to learn my wonderful 66-year-old friend had collapsed and had slipped into a coma. I was driving again by then and I stopped by the Johnson City hospital to check on him on my way over to the High Country.

Mary Ann and Myles' daughter Julie were there. They said there had been no response from him. I stayed with him while they went to get a bite to eat.

After a few minutes, I leaned over Myles' bed and said, "Myles, it's

Nancy." I really didn't expect a response.

"Nancy? Where?" he suddenly said. And then he opened those bright blue eyes, smiled at me, and said, "I love you."

"I love you, too, my friend," I smiled back at him, trying to control my tears.

He closed his eyes and never awoke again. His passing left a hole that will never be filled for those of us (and there were many) who loved him and cherished his good nature and thoughtfulness. He truly enriched our lives.

It is ironic to me that I was so fascinated by the book on Myles Standish when I was a child and that I would have the great privilege of knowing the Myles Standish of my generation.

No other book held that sort of fascination for me. So why, in a totally different part of the country did my path and that of the current generation's Myles Standish cross? What are the odds? Maybe I would have not found the coincidence that I would meet Myles so amazing if I had not treasured the book and story from my childhood.

What a wonderful gift the universe gave me!

14

A Synchronistic Tale of Two Flat Tires

Sometimes you get lucky. Or perhaps your guardian angel keeps an eye out for you. Or maybe the big guy upstairs sends a little help your way just when you need it most. At any rate, I was a very lucky lady indeed several years ago.

It was late afternoon, the paper had been distributed, and I was on the road. I had business at our corporate headquarters in Greeneville, TN, the next day and I was looking forward to spending a rare weekday evening with my husband Bruce at our Greeneville home.

I had passed Roan Mountain and was traveling toward Elizabethton when I heard an ominous "thump-thump-thump" and felt the steering change drastically. Knowing the sound could only be that of a tire going flat, I tried to pull as far off the road as possible. Unfortunately, that section of 19E is a three-lane road with rock on one side and a guardrail on the other. I pulled off as close to the guardrail as I could get, but I was not completely off the road.

It was pouring rain. I had the car loaded down with things I was taking to Greeneville, including my two silver Persian cats that weren't at all impressed with my parking spot and the cars that whizzed by. I got out both of my cell phones only to discover that there was no service on either one. So I sat there for a couple of minutes wondering what in the world I was going to do. Since the car belonged to Bruce, I didn't even know where the spare tire was located. And I knew I was going to get very, very wet while I was trying to find out!

Suddenly, I saw a flashing orange light in my rearview mirror and realized that some sort of big truck had pulled up behind me. A couple of guys got out and walked up to my car window. When I asked who they were, they grinned and said, "We're your good Samaritans!"

Turns out the two men were Eddie Odom and Mark Aldridge, Mountain Electric employees working out of the Roan Mountain office. They were headed back to their office when they saw me with my flat tire and turned around.

These delightful guys didn't make wisecracks (and they were well within their rights to do so) about my filled-to-the-brim car or my very unhappy cats! Instead, they helped me move things and cats so they could get to the jack and the lug wrench, which I would have never found behind the back seat. Then they proceeded, at the risk of their lives, to change my tire. Remember, I said I could not get completely off the road and the flat tire was the front, driver's side tire. It was sitting on the line marking the edge of the road. I stood at the back left corner of my car hoping the cars zooming by would see me and either slow down or move over — preferably both. But the men were actually in the road working, and with the driving rain, the visibility was not good for oncoming traffic.

However, they finished changing the tire without mishap and got the flat tire and all the equipment stowed back where they belonged. Then I tried to pay them for their time and trouble. They flatly refused to take money for their good deed. They merely said, "Just help us out sometime if we have trouble and need it or help someone else you see who might need something." Then they waited and watched me drive out of sight just to make sure I was back on the road and doing okay.

I drove on to Greeneville marveling over how these guys had shown up just when I needed a miracle. Who says miracles don't happen? I owe a big thanks to God and the men from Mountain Electric!

And I have another similar tale of a second flat tire with very similar results. Am I blessed or what?

I either have guardian angels watching over me or I am unbelievably lucky. I have had many situations in my life where miracles happened in the strangest of circumstances and left me shaking my head in wonder.

Of course, one of my best friends in the world for the last 50 years, Alberto Celli (an Italian living near Zurich), swears I need an exorcism because of all the tragedies I have lived through. But we won't go there today! Today is about the good stuff!

When I worked with the newspapers, including the *Mountain Times*, we put out a tourist magazine called the *Summer Times*. In it, we tried to give our summer visitors a lot of ideas about how to have fun (and spend their money!) in the High Country.

In 2003, I had some ideas about a couple of articles for the magazine. I would do a little exploring around our fabulous area and come up with a couple of short auto trips that would be easy and fun and would take the visitor into some of our more remote areas. So, I chose one of the landmarks from my childhood, Sitting Bear near Gingercake Acres. For my other article, I decided I would rediscover Brown Mountain and Brown Mountain Beach that I had visited with my parents when I was a child. Both trips would be away from civilization — but not too far away! At least that's what I thought.

So I started out. I took Highway 181 down the mountain from Pineola and turned on the Gingercake Road, being very careful to check my mileage and write down every landmark for the traveler. Of course, I soon discovered it would have been nice to have a driver, as I kept pulling off to write down something else.

But the trip out to Sitting Bear (which is made up of huge rocks piled on top of each other that, when seen from 181, looks like a big bear hunkered down on top of the mountain) turned out fine.

I took my photographs and all the measurements I needed and eventually came back out on Highway 181.

I was on a roll here! I decided to go ahead and get the other day trip done while I was out. I drove toward Morganton on 181 and, when I got to the bottom of the mountain and the sharp curve near what used to be Clearwater Beach, I turned left and drove until I found the tiny road that runs between the river and Brown Mountain and eventually comes out near the Jonas Ridge Post Office just off Highway 181.

This area, although incredibly beautiful, was much more deserted than I expected. I stopped a lot along the scenic river and took pictures and I jotted down the mileage and made note of landmarks. It took me quite some time before I found myself at the post office in Jonas Ridge. And I did not see a single car the whole way! It was deserted coming up that mountain on a true back road and there was no cell phone service. I was a little uneasy the whole way. But I made it and nothing bad happened.

So I pulled out onto 181, drove a short distance, and had a flat tire! I managed to find a spot that was wide enough to pull off on and I sat there thinking the flat tire could have happened at any point during my trip and I would have been out of luck with no one coming by to find me or help me and no way to contact someone.

I pulled out my cell phone and found, to my dismay, there still was no service. Now what? Maybe I wasn't so lucky after all.

I no sooner had that thought than a car pulled up beside me and a familiar face grinned at me. It was Angie Aldridge. She and her friend were on their way to Morganton when she recognized me and they turned around. They took me to Jim Love's service station near Crossnore. Thankfully, Jim was in and he closed down his station for the length of time it took him to take me to my car, get the tire, bring it back to his shop and fix it, and then go back out and put the tire on my car. He was so nice.

A Synchronistic Tale of Two Flat Tires

Again, luck was either on my side or someone was watching over me! What were the odds in both cases that such instant help would be sent my way? At any rate, I am truly grateful for the help!

15

Synchronicity Stops A Con Artist

It is a little hard to figure out how to write this next tale. Some of the people involved have departed this life. But, although the following is a true story, I am going to have to change the people's names, some of the descriptions, and places in order to protect myself from a very vengeful and diabolical person. I plan to write a fictional book in the near future based on this story and I'll be very careful there also. It is a shame I have to go to these lengths, but law enforcement did not provide any safeguards here and they still don't.

This story also is long, convoluted, and involves lots of incidents of synchronicity. So bear with me, please. It is a very unusual story.

I picked up the phone one day to hear, "You horn in on our territory, you'll be dead in a box!"

Well, that was terrifying. Still, I just thought someone had dialed a wrong number. But that was very unusual.

Then other calls started. One that stands out in my mind was the man who right off the bat said, "How much is it?"

First I must tell you that for a time, I booked musical entertainment in a large city in the northeast. I was married to a bandleader and his bands had lots of overflow bookings that I farmed out to about 40 other bands. I thought it was a shame just to tell people his band was already booked on that date and let them go look for another band. I knew most of the prominent musicians in the area by that time by virtue of being married to one of them. So I opened a musical entertainment agency and lined up many other bands to book for the jobs my husband couldn't play.

Synchronicity Stops A Con Artist

Anyway, back to the story.

"How much is it," he asked.

I immediately said, "How much is what?"

"You know, the entertainment."

"Well," I said, "it depends on what you want. One piece could run you fifty to one hundred dollars. But if you want more pieces, you could pay up to three thousand dollars."

The caller gulped and hung up.

Looking back on the call, it was really funny. In musical entertainment terms, a piece is what we call one musician. Many of the bands we booked were four- or five-piece groups. And sometimes, for big band events, we would book as many as 30 pieces. And, of course, we all know what a "piece" stands for in slang.

I thought the call was very strange, but I didn't connect and didn't understand what was going on.

That is, I didn't understand until I came home one day and my stack of new telephone directories was sitting on my porch. I was excited about seeing them because I couldn't wait to check out my ad. I had splurged and had run a big ad in red with the words "Make Your Party Special!" and I hoped it would bring in lots of new bookings. (It brought things in all right, but not exactly the kind of business I wanted!)

I turned to the entertainment agency section and felt like I had dropped into Alice's rabbit hole. Nothing made sense. Instead of the usual every year grouping of about twelve of us who had been booking musical entertainment for years, there were many, many listings and I had never heard of any of them. I finally found my ad stuck right between The Farmer's Daughter and Gentlemen's VIP.

What on earth?

It finally dawned on me that the listings were for escort and dating services and massage parlors. What was my pretty ad doing in the middle of all that? But now my calls over the last few days made more sense.

I couldn't find out anything. I called my Yellow Page salesperson, who didn't know what had happened. At least that was the story at first. I called the salesperson's supervisor and got stonewalled there. She refused to talk about it.

I finally found out what happened from a friend who was a policeman. He told me the dating and escort services and the massage parlors were, for the most part, fronts for prostitution and law enforcement had asked the telephone company to remove the headings, "Dating Services," "Escort Services," and "Massage Parlors" from their categories for the thick Yellow Pages book. Apparently, the telephone company got greedy. There were nearly one hundred listings under these categories. I was told that the same people contract for many telephone numbers with a central location and list them under different agencies with different ads.

That didn't help my situation much, but it did explain why I was getting the weird calls.

I called the heads of the other agencies. What did we do about the situation? We went to see the supervisor who had refused to talk with us. By this time, all the legitimate agencies were upset and I'm sure she had had calls from most of them. She agreed to talk with us.

I had a solution, I thought. If she would just send out a several page addendum to the Yellow Pages that could be slipped into the book with only the legitimate musical entertainment agencies, we would accept that fix. She flatly refused. So we left very angry. (This woman was fired a few weeks later for her poor handling of

Synchronicity Stops A Con Artist

the situation.)

Since the telephone company wasn't going to take any action, we had to see what we could do. We had a couple of meetings of all twelve of the entertainment agencies. We took various solutions. The telephone company finally offered a year's free advertising if we didn't pursue the matter further. Most of the agencies took the deal.

I had a different problem. My agency was in my home. I had a child in the home. The threats were scary as anyone could get my address from my business license. Another of the agency owners had the same situation. We decided not to settle because the offered solution left us in a dangerous position. She and I decided to sue.

Her name was Dorcas and she and I became pretty well acquainted as we strategized and tried to figure out what to do. The case played out over the next year or so and I won't go into the outcome both because there is a gag order on the trial and it really is not germane to the rest of my story. But it does set the background. If I had not had the problem and worked with Dorcas to settle it, I would never have known her well and there would not have been the incredible instances of synchronicity that revealed themselves over the course of the next months.

Dorcas had a good friend she worked with in her business. Lucas was an excellent musician and, in fact, I had booked him myself a couple of times. Dorcas shared more and more of her life as I got to know her better. Finally, she told me that her friend Lucas had been fighting possibly terminal cancer for months and she and her husband were giving him as much money for his very expensive experimental treatments as they could spare. Dorcas was terribly worried about him.

Then she told me something that made me very suspicious. She said that Lucas had been in love with her for several years, but since she was married and would never break her wedding vows, they could never act on their feelings and their love would be unrequited forever.

As I said, I booked Lucas a couple of times. Actually, Lucas and I had never met. I always arranged the bookings over the phone. Sometimes I booked him and his significant other, Danny, and it was general knowledge among area musicians that the two shared a gay relationship and had been together for a number of years. So Lucas was NOT pining away over his love for Dorcas. But how did I tell her? She had no idea.

I had this great idea. I asked her if Lucas could possibly have HIV. This question offended Dorcas at first and then she called later and asked if I thought he was gay. I told her what I knew about his relationship with Danny. She started considering the possibility. She really had not known.

Here we have the first instance of synchronicity. I knew Danny pretty well as I had booked him a lot and he was part of the group of mainstream musicians that played in the area in various bands. If I had not been involved with Dorcas over the Yellow Pages problem and learned she believed Lucas was in love with her, she would have continued to believe he was.

Then another puzzle piece fell into place. Dorcas told me that Lucas had recently borrowed $1,000 from her so he could pay for new dresses from an upscale area department store for his mother and his aunt to wear to attend one of his concerts. She said his uncle had taken part in a pyramid scheme, got caught, and had to declare bankruptcy. His mother and his aunt needed dresses to wear and they couldn't afford to buy them for themselves. Dorcas mentioned their names.

I KNEW BOTH HIS MOTHER AND HIS AUNT! They lived in a small town several hundred miles away and I had also lived there at one time years earlier. I had worked with both ladies! I also knew

Synchronicity Stops A Con Artist

about the uncle's bankruptcy. It had occurred while I was living and working there twenty years earlier. Lucas was presenting his uncle's troubles as though they were a recent occurrence. They weren't.

So, I called Lucas' aunt whom I knew well. We had been friends and I often had visited in her home. We had a very long conversation about Lucas. By this time, I had discovered several other schemes Lucas was running on other people and I told my old friend everything I knew. The aunt told me that she and Lucas' mother had never attended one of his concerts and that he had never bought them dresses. So I caught Lucas in another lie, thanks to synchronicity.

Lucas' aunt called his mother and told her all I had said. Lucas' mother called him and took him to task over his wrongdoings. He was furious at Dorcas for telling me anything and, in fact, was so angry with me that I feared for my safety. I was glad he had never met me in person during the course of our interactions.

What were the odds that I would know both Lucas' aunt and mother from years before in a totally different location? What were the odds that I was around for the bankruptcy and knew when it had actually happened? The whole thing was just too bizarre. I was the only person in the whole city, or possibly the country, who had these pieces of the puzzle and enough information to connect them. As more things came to light, I became firmly convinced that I was pulled into the situation in order to help Dorcas, who was planning to give any money she received from the Yellow Pages fiasco to Lucas for more experimental cancer treatments. But the tale continues.

I got much more of the story out of Lucas' partner, Danny. Since I knew him quite well, I had no problem pushing him for information on Lucas. When he realized how much I knew about Lucas and his nefarious schemes and cons, Danny finally told me what he knew. I asked him point blank if Lucas were conning Dorcas and he answered, "Yeah, I'm afraid he is." Reluctantly, he told me the whole story.

Danny was a young, impressionable sixteen-year-old when he met Lucas, who persuaded him that it was God's will that they have a gay partnership. Danny believed him. Danny also told me of the many times Lucas had conned people or stolen things and gotten them both into trouble. Finally, Lucas changed his name and had been using "Lucas" for a number of years to avoid prosecution in other states. Of course, I told Dorcas everything I had learned. She now believed everything I said.

Then I had another instance of synchronicity. Just before all of Lucas' schemes came to light, Lucas had asked Dorcas for money for an experimental cancer treatment that required him to fly in a doctor, Dr. Michael Longstreet from Cedars of Lebanon/Mount Sinai Hospital in New York. He said the treatments were totally illegal, but Dr. Longstreet was willing to do it for Lucas. Dorcas paid for everything and Dr. Longstreet was flown in.

Interestingly, I visited with my stepson a week or so later and I asked him what he had been doing lately. I could not believe his answer. He said a visiting musician named Michael Longstreet had come to town to play a gig and he had asked my stepson, a musician, to work with him.

"Michael Longstreet?" I asked. "Longstreet is an unusual name. Is he from New York City?"

"Yes, he just flew in from New York for the job."

I asked him if Lucas was present at the job and my stepson told me that he was there.

The rather extraordinary incident of synchronicity gave me the truth about the "doctor" from New York. It was just another scam. I told Dorcas and she was very upset. But she knew now that the

Synchronicity Stops A Con Artist

man who professed to love her was a criminal con artist.

Again, the fates—or synchronicity—had dropped the truth right in my lap. It was like the universe just shoved all the pieces in my direction. Frankly, no one else in the world had all this information and could have put it together. Although I couldn't save the probably $500,000 Dorcas already had spent on Lucas, I did keep her from getting scammed further, much to Lucas' displeasure.

There was so much more to this story. We really started looking into things and found many more instances where Lucas had conned so many people. Between fifty and sixty older women in a church where he played the organ were sending him money each month to pay for his "treatments." He had huge parties with champagne fountains, all at Dorcas' expense. He sold the same items to several different people. There were so many schemes. We really felt something could be done legally. It was not to be. Gifts don't count and, cunningly, everything Lucas took could have been construed as a "gift." While the whole thing was fraud, when Dorcas contacted the FBI, SBI, and the Secret Service to see if they could help, they would not. She was told that if she wanted to spend an additional $50,000 and hire a private investigator to compile evidence, they might be interested. She had spent too much and she couldn't afford to spend more.

About that time, Lucas moved away. Interestingly, there was one more major bit of synchronicity that showed up.

Dorcas called me one day and said she had just heard an interesting ad on the radio. One of the churches in a nearby town had bought a new organ and the music store that sold the organ to the church was flying in a very special musician to present a concert on the new acquisition the following weekend. The public was invited. The special musician was Lucas!

"We have to go," Dorcas said.

So we did. Ironically, I also knew the owner of the music store who handled the sale of the organ. So I disguised myself with a wig, different makeup, dark glasses, and flashy clothing. I wasn't too worried about Lucas recognizing me as he had never met me in person, but I wasn't taking any chances. Dorcas, of course, couldn't disguise herself so Lucas wouldn't recognize her, so she went early and hid in the balcony.

I sat in my car watching for Lucas' arrival and I wasn't disappointed. However, I was surprised. My friend from the music store was holding on to Lucas who was wearing dark glasses and tapping around with a white cane. Another scheme! Lucas was pretending to be blind!

I got a seat near the front of the church and listened while Lucas gave his concert. He truly was a gifted musician and could have earned much money honestly without resorting to the cons. In the middle of his concert, he stood up and told the audience how he had been affected by this horrible ailment and that it was only through the goodness of people like the owner of the music store flying him various places to do concerts that he was able to survive. He told them that he was playing for the glory of God and people started pressing money on him from all sides of the church.

I went out to my car and took a number of pictures of my friend helping Lucas back to his car so he could take him to the airport for a flight out. I had the pictures developed at a one-hour photo place.

On Monday morning when the music store opened, I was there with the pictures. I spread them out on my friend's desk and said, "Do I have a story to tell you!"

I proceeded to tell him the whole story of Lucas and his schemes. My friend got paler and paler. It turned out that my friend had promised to ship on consignment—no money exchanged until later— a $60,000 pipe organ to Lucas in another state the very next morning. He would have never seen a penny of that money. I stopped him from doing that and he was always grateful.

"I will find some reason why I can't ship that organ," he told me. He totally cut ties with Lucas and never hired him again.

Again, an owner of just any music store might not have listened to my tale, but I had known this man for years and he knew I was telling him the truth. Synchronicity again!

While I wish I could say that this man is no longer a danger to unsuspecting and trusting people, I can't. He is still out there and, apparently, he has been slick enough to have avoided the law.

16

Chance Question Synchronicity

Every now and then, a very small event triggers a huge sequence of events. One wonders if any of the events would have happened without the trigger. Is the trigger synchronicity? You can be the judge!

Sometimes we get lucky. Sometimes life hands us wonderful situations and experiences and friends whether we deserve them or not. We certainly have all experienced life's "curve balls" when things didn't turn out as expected. Sometimes these unexpected turns aren't very pleasant. Occasionally these little (or big) surprises bring big miracles to one's life. I had a very big and extremely meaningful surprise a few years ago that I would like to share with you. Most of the people in my true story are no longer with us, so sharing it won't affect anyone adversely at this point.

In 1995, my father, Odes Stroupe, was a semi-invalid paralyzed from a stroke he had the week after my mother died in 1992. He couldn't do much in terms of physical activity, but he enjoyed going to the Senior Center and seeing old friends there.

One day, he came home very agitated. He was a bit ashamed to share what had happened with me, but since I was the only one around to listen, he didn't have much choice and he really had to talk. He told me that he had asked a lady he had dated a year or so before he married my mother about her children. When she started telling him about her daughter, she said, "By the way, she's yours."

His chance question turned into a really astonishing surprise. My father was both excited and dubious. The daughter in question was 60 years old and lived in Burlington. My father tried to figure out when everything had happened to see if it were possible for him to be the father. He was doubtful and mentioned his doubts to the lady at the Senior Center the next day. She wouldn't talk about the daughter after that and she died a couple of months later. She had known she had a terminal illness and I guess she finally decided to tell him after all those years.

So Dad and I went to the funeral to see if we could satisfy our curiosity about the daughter. Her name was Joyce and she was standing in the receiving line between her two younger brothers.

Dad put out his hand and said, "I'm Odes Stroupe."

Joyce took his hand in both of hers and said, "I know who you are."

Such simple phrases to convey so much. As I looked at the two of them standing there, I was struck by the resemblance between them. She looked a lot more like my father than I did!

I finally got up my nerve and asked Joyce if I could call her in a few days. She said she thought we ought to talk and gave me her phone number in Burlington. I tried to make myself call her for two weeks and couldn't manage to do it. I kept thinking that if Dad were her father, it would change everything I had always thought to be true. I would be the middle child instead of the oldest. Part of me wanted to deny that she could be my sister and keep things the way they always had been. But the question had been raised and it wasn't going to disappear.

Finally Joyce called me. I told her I had a question to ask her and I didn't know how to ask it. She told me she thought she knew what I was going to ask and just to go ahead.

I hesitatingly asked, "Are we related?"

And she said, "Yes, I think we might be."

So we made an appointment for her to come talk with my father and me the next day.

The meeting was awkward at first. We were strangers to each other. Dad still didn't believe she could be his daughter. He felt he would have heard about her from someone over the years if it were true. Joyce had always been told he was her father and she thought all those years that he had known about her and had rejected her.

I wondered why I hadn't heard about her sometime while I was growing up. Kids can be cruel. But I had heard nothing. We later found that my Uncle Hoke (who was a close friend of Joyce's mother) had known about it. Also, my aunt, Elizabeth Sloop, knew and said Sam Brown had told her several years earlier, but she didn't really believe it. And Harold Moldenhauer, one of Dad's best friends, said he had heard it years earlier, but he never mentioned it to my father.

We all decided a DNA test was in order to settle the matter. My father was worried because he was afraid the test would show that he wasn't Joyce's father and then she would have no one to help her figure out who her father really was. Dad liked her a lot and, by this time, was hoping she wouldn't be disappointed.

An additional bit of synchronicity—one of Joyce's daughters worked for a geneticist at Roche Laboratories in Burlington and her boss offered to do the test for free and put it at the top of her list. How very convenient was that?

A few weeks later, Joyce called and told me excitedly that the test had come back positive. "He's my pop!" she said.

So, I had a sister. I'll have to tell you that by that time, I really didn't need a DNA test to convince me. Joyce and I had quickly developed an incredibly strong bond. We had both always wanted a sister and had felt something was missing in our lives. Even our personalities were very similar. I never had any problem figuring out a gift for her. I just bought what I would like and she loved it. She soon became my very best friend. I would have been heartbroken if the results had not been positive. She had three great daughters that I instantly loved and grandchildren I adored.

Over the next three years, Joyce and Dad spent a lot of time together and tried to make up for all the years apart. She took him to Burlington for a few days and served him breakfast in bed. Since she had a vacation cabin near me, they came often to visit. She and Dad grew to love each other deeply. I regret that they had only three years together before Dad died. When he did die, Joyce and I were there for each other. It was a great comfort.

A chance question, a tiny bit of synchronicity, brought a miracle seemingly created from nowhere! I had a wonderful sister who suddenly appeared out of the blue when I had been in this world for five decades. I had her for four more years after my father died. We could not have been closer if we had always been in each other's life. When Bruce and I met and fell in love, Joyce was delighted with my choice. She was going to be my matron of honor.

A week before the wedding, Joyce and her husband Lon had come to their cabin near Spruce Pine to entertain some friends from Mississippi and to finalize plans for the wedding. Joyce had found the perfect dress and we spent the afternoon talking about our plans. Joyce and Bruce kept calling each other "Bro" and "Sis." It was funny and delightful. Joyce did say she had a headache, but we were having fun and she seemed to be okay.

Then we went to an outdoor music venue on a mountain to hear some bluegrass music and had just arrived when Joyce suddenly stumbled and started slurring her words. We rushed her to the hospital where she immediately was flown on to Johnson City Medical Center. She had had a massive stroke and she died early the next morning.

We debated for a while about canceling the wedding, but Joyce's daughters insisted that they were there and their mother would be unhappy if we didn't carry on. So we did.

We had Joyce's funeral on Friday and Bruce and I were married on Saturday. Lon gave me away and Joyce's daughter Judy took her place in the wedding. We had a tribute to Joyce during the ceremony. I had never before experienced such feelings of great joy mixed with such feelings of deep sadness.

And there is my story, put into play by a chance question from my dad at the Senior Center. Life threw me a big curve, but it brought me great joy and still does. I am so grateful to have had my wonderful sister even for such a short time. I still have her lovely family and now it is my family, too.

Joyce and I were so tickled that we told our tale to anyone who would listen! We were proud of each other and the fact that we were sisters. There was no room for shame and bigoted recriminations in the love two grateful sisters shared with each other and their wonderful father.

It is an experience I would never have had without the intervention of a little synchronicity. I would have missed out on so much if Dad hadn't asked a chance question. I'm so glad he did!

17

Manifesting

Synchronicity accounts for many of my minor and major miracles, but there seems to be a little something else at play. My daughter has always said I was good at manifesting things I wanted. And who knows? Maybe I am. Sometimes, perhaps I am too good! (I get what I wish for and find I don't want it after all!)

A lot of books have been written on the art of manifesting in recent years. In fact, many people have built an entire career on teaching people the "art" of manifesting.

What is manifesting? It is holding in your mind a vision of what you want to come into physical form and most of the people who claim to be experts in the area suggest that you have to act like you already have what you seek, so you open a path to pull that desired object or happening into your life. Not to be a spoilsport here, but when I hear this statement, I get the image of driving down the road in a car you don't have yet! A little tricky, to say the least! But perhaps you can drive in your mind's eye and not out on the pavement!

Manifesting does seem to work. I can't deny that I occasionally have something show up in my life that I cannot explain away at all. The following is an example:

I had this wonderful idea. Terra cotta pots retain heat a bit. What, I thought, if I paint the pots, put rubber or cork on the bottom to protect any surface, and put a coordinating square of material inside the pot that would tie or loop through a ring for closure? The pot, which I very originally called the "Bread Pot," would be a nice addition to the table and would keep the bread warm during the meal.

I remembered that a few years before, I had read about a terra cotta kit that could be used for actually baking bread. Thinking that would be a good place to start with my idea to see just what I needed to do, I looked and looked for a kit like I remembered seeing. I couldn't find anything.

A day or two later, I took my trash to a dump other than the one I usually used, but it was close to my studio and convenient that day. Actually, I think that was the only time I ever went to that trash dump.

I dumped my bags of trash and started walking back to my car. Suddenly, I caught sight of a terra cotta pot sitting on a retaining wall near the dumpsters. People apparently used this wall to leave something that was too good to put in the trash in hopes that someone would see it and want it.

I walked over to the pot to see just what it was. It was completely wrapped in cellophane with the labels still on and had never been opened. It was a brand new terra cotta bread baking kit complete with all the supplies and ingredients and instructions!

I have noticed through the years that sometimes I seemed to be able to "think" something into existence. Perhaps it was just coincidence, but maybe it was actually manifesting.

The subjects of manifesting and "your thoughts create your future" have always intrigued me. I guess it all started with Napoleon Hill and his blockbuster book of the early Twentieth Century (1937, I believe), *Think and Grow Rich*. Several decades ago, I first heard of the book. I read it. In the years since, I've read many other books based on this book and its theories.

Anyway, it made a difference in my life and the way I thought about the world. The premise, that your thoughts are the forerunners and the necessary building blocks for your future (my interpretation, not necessarily Napoleon Hill's!), made an immediate impression.

Manifesting

It was an idea that made me say, "Aha! Yes, I think that is true."

So I went on to study many New Age writers and then I delved back into the ancient Eastern sources of the New Age gurus. It was all very interesting indeed.

I made the acquaintance of Wayne Dyer, Deepak Chopra, Louise Hay, Michael Newton, Marianne Williamson, and many other present day philosophers who look at our world just a bit differently.

From each one, I learned. Dr. Wayne Dyer was a mentor for me. He was a source of inspiration, a wellspring of ideas, and the calming voice of common sense in the midst of worldly confusion.

When Wayne gave a seminar in Asheville, NC, I attended. I managed to speak with him after the program. I told him of a lucid dream I had had (the one recounted in Chapter 22 in this book) and the things it taught me. He was very interested. He asked me to write down all the details and send it to him in an envelope marked with a big red Sharpie star. I did so and, a few weeks later, I received a big box from Wayne full of autographed copies of his books! (Of course I was now even more impressed with Dr. Wayne Dyer!)

I became fascinated with quantum theory, both from Stephen Hawking (the brilliant Harvard theoretical physicist who had Lou Gehrig's Disease) and also Dr. Deepak Chopra, whose interpretation comes by way of India, where he grew up.

Lately, I've been very interested in *The Secret*, a movie that was put together by a number of self-help teachers, including Bob Proctor, John Gray (*Men are from Mars/Women are from Venus*), Jack Canfield (*Chicken Soup for the Soul*), and many other inspirational speakers.

The Secret again is based on the premise that your thoughts create your future. These thinkers call it the "Law of Attraction" and believe that you can attract into your life just about anything you want if you believe it strongly enough.

I agree. I've had many experiences that have given me reason to believe this premise. For instance, some years ago I typed out two pages detailing just what I wanted in a husband or mate. I was very specific and quite detailed. I told myself I would find such a person, but life went on and I eventually forgot I had made that list. One day, a couple of years after I married Bruce, I found the list. As I read it, I was filled with wonder. It was Bruce—absolutely and down to the last detail! I had "ordered" Bruce!

That is just one incident. There have been many more such occurrences in my life.

Of course, somebody is always bound to say, "Be careful what you wish for. You just might get it!"

As with synchronicity, manifesting seems to happen with unrelated events. There doesn't seem to be any connection with what you want and how you get it. I like to think of the old-fashioned chenille bedspread. When I was a child, I would lie on the spread and look at the small "nubs" that sat, raised, on the surface. If I lay my head down so I looked across the little sea of nubs, it looked like a lot of individual little bumps that were not connected. However, the background fabric connected them all and they were all a part of the overall pattern. I think we are like that bedspread. We seem to be totally unconnected, but life in general and perhaps the fabric of the universe connect us to each other and the overall picture.

I remember hearing of an experiment with particles done many years ago that confirmed that there was some kind of connection between these particles that we don't understand and can't begin to figure out why. At least at that point in time, physicists were quite puzzled. I think I read about this sometime in the late seventies, so I don't know if it was ever figured out or not.

Anyway, I believe the particles were photons of light and they were matched particles spinning in the same direction. They were moved to a distance of several miles apart and, when some sort of stimulus was applied to one of the particles to change its direction, the particle that was in the remote location also changed its spin simultaneously to match. So, there obviously is some sort of long-range quantum connection between these particles that we don't understand. Are we also connected on some quantum level or in some other and as yet undiscovered way? Such a connection would not surprise me and would help to account for both synchronicity and the art of manifesting.

Sometimes making a "vision board" is a good way to facilitate your attempts to manifest whatever you want. An empowering vision board provides an actual, physical reminder of the things you want to see in your life and keeps your focus on these things. Police departments use evidence boards, link charts, or investigation boards sometimes to lay out their cases and to clarify what is known and which way to proceed. You can do much the same thing with your vision board. Call it anything you wish, a postulate board, a wish board, or something else.

I would recommend your putting pictures of everything you want to manifest in your life on the board. Keep old magazines handy so you can cut them up for pictures for your board.

Vision boards can be very fancy or very plain. Taylor yours to your own style. You can use a commercially made cork bulletin board or you can make a board from poster board or display foam board or from anything else you like. Your creation can be any size you like, but be sure to make one that is big enough to contain all your desires.

Print and paste on your board words that reflect your goals—even whole sentences. The whole point is to remind you of exactly the things you are trying to bring into your life. Some such words are: success, money, love, happiness, joy, and riches. You can also list desires such as: I publish a book or I buy a beautiful new house.

The closer your pictures on your vision board match your desires, the easier it will be to manifest them.

Look at your board several times a day. Say some of the words you pasted on out loud so your subconscious mind "gets" the picture—literally! Your vision board will be too big to take with you, but there is an easy way to manage just that. Take a picture with your phone or print out a picture from a camera and carry it with you where you can access that picture several times a day. Be sure to repeat your goals.

Also remember that when manifesting things, many self-help teachers believe that vibration levels attract similar levels of things that can be manifested, so for loftier goals and desires, concentrate on positive energy and good thoughts.

I remember reading about a woman who really wanted a new house. One day, while she was turning through a magazine, she saw a picture of a house she loved. She cut out the picture and put it on her vision board. Every day she looked at the picture of the house. She saw herself in her mind owning that house. She imagined how she would decorate the house. She made it hers. A short time later, she met a man on a dating site and they started seeing each other. When the relationship became serious and they decided to marry, the man found a house he thought his wife-to-be would like and he took her to see it. I don't think any of you reading will be surprised when I tell you that the house he took her to see was the *actual house* in her picture! And since she had never shown him her vision board, he had no way of knowing about the house she loved.

Always remember that we are all connected to our source and that we are divine creations. There are no accidents; everything happens for a reason. We do have to envision and ask for our heart's desires.

18

A Little Manifesting of My Own

A few years ago, I was sitting outside in my yard enjoying the pleasant mountain sunshine. I didn't have a lot on my mind and it felt really good to relax.

As I sat there, my eye fell on a piece of shingle material that apparently had fallen off the roof and was lying on the ground beside the house. Curious, I got up and walked over to the piece of shingle and picked it up. It looked like it had broken off from the roof so I tried to see if there was any damage to the roof. When I took a good look at my roof, I realized that many of the shingles had a bit of damage. Although I didn't have any leaks yet, it certainly was a matter of time before I would if I didn't soon replace the roof.

I was not in any shape to replace a roof! I was newly divorced and had moved to my old (literally) childhood home in the mountains with my daughter. We couldn't swing a new roof any time soon. Oh well.

I kept thinking about the roof. Then I realized I was making myself a bit crazy obsessing about the roof and that was doing no good at all. So, I said to myself, "I have a brand new roof," and I envisioned the roof with all new shingles shining in the sunlight. And then I forgot the whole thing!

A couple of months later, I got a call from one of my old friends with whom I had grown up. I had not seen Paul in several years. He moved out of state shortly after we left school. We chatted and caught up for a few minutes and then he changed the subject.

"I have a really good friend," he said, "who is in a mess and really needs someone to talk it out with. Can I give him your number?" I agreed to try to help, having been a psychotherapist for some years in another life, and the friend, Dave, called me for the first of a series of phone calls where he talked about the disaster he was living through, which was no fault of his own.

As it turned out, Dave was a professor of technology at a major university. His wife had gone back to graduate school and, over the course of a year or so, had gotten involved romantically with the head of her department—a *married* head of her department! The professor's wife found out about his affair with his student and she shot and killed both the professor and herself. Dave's wife, feeling very guilty for her part in the situation, confessed everything to Dave and then moved out. Dave was blindsided. He didn't see any of it coming and really thought his marriage was fine. He and his wife were both very busy with teaching and school. His life had fallen totally apart and he was left wondering what happened, how it happened, and how he would deal with everything.

We talked for a couple of hours at a time several times a week for several months. Dave gradually came to accept what had happened and found ways to move on. He dealt with all the chaos and got his life back, perhaps even better than it was before. One weekend, he came to see me to thank me. He was a great guy and, in fact, became a good friend. I still hear from him occasionally. But I digress.

Before he left to return to his university, I noticed he was outside walking around the house. I didn't think anything about it other than I figured he needed some fresh air and exercise. A little later, he came to tell me goodbye and take his leave. What he said next just floored me.

"You need a new roof. That is how I'm going to repay you for being so nice, listening to my problems, and helping me so much. I will come for the next several weekends and I'll get your roof put on. What color do you want?"

A Little Manifesting of My Own

Wow! I didn't see that coming. "You really would put on a new roof?" I asked in total surprise.

"I do some special project each summer for someone who has a need as my way of giving back. And you are going to be this summer's project. I teach technology, for goodness sakes! I'm good at this. It is what I teach and I need to be 'hands on' for a while each year."

And, true to his word, Dave came every weekend and worked on my roof. He brought all the materials and the tools. After several weekend trips, I had a beautiful (extremely well-constructed) new roof. He would not let me pay for anything. I will be grateful forever. My thought or desire that I just released and forgot had very powerful manifesting qualities apparently! No one was more surprised than I was that it worked!

19

Manifesting a Husband

Not too long ago, I was going through some boxes of papers, notebooks, and files from years before and trying to clear some room in my storage area. You know how it is when something catches your eye and, before you know it, you are totally immersed in the past and your memories. Well, I was.

I found old recipes, old articles I had written for various things, old letters from friends, and much more. Then, as I pulled out another stack of papers, a folded piece of notepaper fell to the floor. I picked it up and opened it.

It was a shopping list—for a husband! I was not in a relationship at the time and I had decided just exactly what qualities I wanted in a husband, so I made a list.

My list included: friendship, good sense of humor, trustworthy, dependable, kind, having integrity, and respect. I also added things like having a lot of things in common, such as the things we enjoyed doing and mutual values. I wanted someone who was intelligent and who made a good living. Yeah, I know money isn't everything, but it usually is an indicator of success and I did want a successful man!

When I read over the list, I was stunned. My husband, Bruce, whom I had met years after I penned my "want" list, had EVERY SINGLE QUALITY I had put on the list! Every one!

How was that possible? I told Bruce that I had "special ordered" him!

While we are on the subject of Bruce and my "order," let me tell you

Manifesting a Husband

a little more about how we met and what happened. It did involve some more manifesting, but there was a lot of synchronicity also, and perhaps a miracle or two!

When I met Bruce, I was working as the general manager of a newspaper in the mountains of North Carolina. Every Monday I would go over to the next county to the paper's headquarters to take my ads and copy for the week so they could be put into the paper that was printed there.

On this particular day, I was upstairs near the balcony that overlooked the main entry when the paper's owner walked in with a huge bundle of inflated balloons.

"I won the lottery," he announced to the building at large. "Well, not really," he said. "I sold the newspaper. The suits are coming in an hour or so."

The "suits" did come shortly. Our paper staff tended toward hippyish dress and attitude and the three men who paid us a visit that day were indeed dressed in suits. They were the top executives from the Tennessee-based newspaper group that was buying our papers. One of the men was Bruce, who was the chief operating officer and who ran the company that employed about 550 employees. Another was his second in command. The third man was to be taking over the North Carolina area papers as the area vice president.

I met all three men. I confess, they seemed a bit old for me to be interested, but perhaps that was because of their air of competency, more than their actual ages.

The next Wednesday, I was back at headquarters for a meeting with the new owners again as we had to sign up for benefits and learn the new company rules and policies. I was sitting there filling out paperwork.

Bruce suddenly walked over to me and said, "You are left-handed. Are you an artist?"

I didn't know what to make of his question, but I answered that I was.

"My wife is left-handed and an artist," he said, "and she has this strange condition where she sees numbers and letters in color."

"Synesthesia?" I asked him. "I have that and my daughter does, too."

Until December of 1999 when *Discover* magazine carried an article about synesthesia, I believed everybody thought fives were yellow and tens were blue—that is, when I gave it any thought at all! I didn't realize my perceptions and thought processes were a little different from the norm. (Please, no smart remarks here!)

I am one of a group of people who have a condition called "synesthesia." The term refers to a related set or complex of various cognitive states having in common that stimuli to one sense (such as smell) are involuntarily simultaneously perceived as if by one or more other senses (such as sight and/or hearing). For instance, many synesthetes see certain colors when they hear music and, usually, each instrument's sound will produce a consistent color. There are other people who taste words, feel sounds, or see pain in color.

The most common type of synesthesia is the colored letter/number type, such as I have. Estimates run anywhere from 1 in 500 people who have this type to 1 in 3,000 who have colored musical sounds. For those who taste things they touch or have multiple forms of synesthesia, the condition affects perhaps 1 in 15,000.

About 70 percent of synesthetes are female and many of those are left-handed. A large number of the left-handed female synesthetes also have artistic or musical talents. (I am female, left-handed, and an artist!)

In the most common type, the colored written letter characters (graphemes), numbers, time units, and musical notes or keys, the grapheme is always seen as the same color, even over the course of many years. My yellow fives and blue tens have always been those colors.

Some synesthetes see the color in their mind's eye or on a screen in their head. For others, the colors are so vivid they actually see them floating several feet in front of them. The colors come involuntarily, although many synesthetes "tune out" the colors when reading. Texture is also associated with letters or numbers for many people. For instance, many people see A as a bright apple red color. For some, it is slick and shiny or shaded and opaque for others.

There are many theories about what causes synesthesia. Since the regions of the brain that normally produce these sensations are in close proximity, many researchers are speculating that there is some sort of "overflow" that occurs. Whether it is a connection that should have disappeared shortly after infancy or whether it is an added or abnormal connection is not understood yet.

CBS's *60 Minutes* one year ran a program on synesthesia and featured a woman who felt sounds and a man who tasted words. A popular book on the subject is *The Man Who Tasted Shapes* by Richard Cytowic.

Although non-synesthetes tend to view the condition as abnormal and troublesome, I wouldn't want to give up what I consider to be a gift. I use the condition as a handy filing system and I find it helps to match colors either in a painting or in a clothing store! If I can't remember a name or a word, I can usually remember the color it is and I can sort through my mental file of names or words that are that color and find the one I want. For me, the world is a wonderfully colored experience and I treasure it as such!

But let me get back to my story. Bruce pulled out his cell phone, called his wife, Julie, and said, "I found one! Her name is Nancy and she is left-handed, an artist, and has synesthesia!"

I learned both Bruce and Julie had been looking for other synesthetes. Julie had synesthesia and they didn't know anyone else with the condition.

He handed the phone to me and Julie and I spent about an hour talking, comparing our synesthesia and our various letters and their colors, and made tentative plans to meet in several weeks. I was excited because, other than my daughter, I didn't know any other synesthetes, either.

The next Monday found me back at headquarters turning in my ads and articles for the week as usual. I noticed everyone seemed very subdued and nobody was talking. The people in this office never stopped talking and joking. What was up? I finally asked.

One of the reporters (who had been there on Wednesday of last week when I had the long call with Julie) spoke up. "You remember the lady you talked with for so long last week? Bruce's wife? Well, some kids were racing Friday night, lost control of their car, and hit Bruce and Julie head on. She died instantly."

I was stunned. No wonder nobody felt like talking. It made me sick. How awful!

"How is Bruce?" I asked. I was told that he had a concussion, but was out of the hospital and doing okay.

I continued to ask about Bruce when anyone came our way from our new home office in Tennessee. He gradually got better, but Julie's loss had devastated him. They had been married for twenty years.

A couple of weeks later, I was returning home from a trip to

Charlotte. For some reason, when I started driving up the mountain from Morganton, thoughts of Julie popped into my head.

I said aloud, "Julie, I'm really sorry we never got to meet. It would have been a colorful meeting! I know Bruce is hurting. If there is anything I can do for him, please let me know. I'll help in any way I can."

A couple of hours later, I sat down at my home computer and, to my surprise, found an e-mail from Bruce. It read, "I'm really sorry you and Julie never got to meet. It would have been a colorful meeting! I would like to come over this weekend and see our new properties in the High Country. Would you be available to take me around?"

I got goose bumps! The hairs on the back of my neck stood up! What were the odds? The same exact language? How could that happen? Was Julie speaking to me or was it just a huge, strange coincidence?

I wrote Bruce back and, the following weekend, I showed him around the High Country. We talked about my talking with Julie while driving up the mountain and finding the same words in his e-mail. Neither of us could figure out how Bruce got my home e-mail. The business e-mail address was pretty easily obtainable for him. But my personal one? I didn't remember giving it to Julie, but I possibly could have done so. Bruce didn't remember how he had gotten it, either. It was very strange.

Anyway, he came back the next weekend. We found we enjoyed each other's company, liked many of the same things and activities, and had the same values. We spent endless hours talking and finally started talking every night on the phone for a couple of hours.

Before long, we met halfway between our houses. That was an hour's drive for both of us. We had a nice dinner and visited. He finally invited me to his home in Tennessee to meet all his animals. He had met all of mine!

Going to his home was another very strange experience. His animals loved me. Well, except for the black devil cat, Schatzi! She didn't like Julie, either.

But the shock came when I looked into the room Julie used for her office/studio. We had 50 to 60 of the very same books. We had the same art supplies—pastels, oils, watercolors, acrylics—even the same exact sets. We had the same jewelry-making tools and the same brands of supplies. I happened to look up on one of her walls and there, framed, was my very favorite poem, "Invictus." She had the same computer equipment and the same how-to books for all the equipment. She was a writer, a jewelry maker, a seamstress, an artist. And so was I! She even had a shawl woven in my tiny hometown! *I had a duplicate studio in my own house.*

Again, what are the odds? It was a seamless fit for everything and later that year, we married and I fitted right in as though everything were made for me—and perhaps it was!

20

Gratitude

The more grateful you are,
the more you become, achieve, and obtain.

One thing that the philosophers, both New Age and ancient Eastern, have in common is a belief in the necessity of being grateful. I call it an "attitude of gratitude."

For some reason, gratitude seems to complete the manifesting cycle. It is "your part" of the process. When God and the universe give to you, your gratitude is your response. All of the philosophers I have mentioned previously recommend making a list of the things for which you are grateful.

Rhonda Byrne even puts out *The Secret Gratitude Journal*. I have a copy. I got it years ago and, although I did not use it as much as I intended, I enjoyed the little tips for being grateful she put in on most pages.

I also have published my own *The Magic Within Journal*, which is divided into sections and is a great place to record your feelings of gratitude, together with your own synchronicities and miracles, your dreams, your manifesting goals, your postulates, and your affirmations. Look for it on Amazon or where you bought this book.

Writing down the things for which we are grateful reminds us to count our blessings. I find I am even more blessed than I realize when I take stock in this manner. We tend to go through our lives taking a lot of things for granted. A gratitude list makes us stop and appreciate. A gratitude list can make us feel really good. And it helps us meet every single day with gratefulness.

I keep a permanent list of the things for which I am *always* grateful. I go over this list every night before I go to sleep, just to remind myself how lucky I am. This list helps a lot if I am tired or a little down or feeling discouraged.

Then, most evenings, I also make a list of the small things that have happened during the day and for which I am grateful. If there is something of momentous importance on this list and for which I will continue to be very grateful, I add it to my permanent list. This system works well for me and makes me really appreciate all the neat things, events, and people that come into my life on a daily basis. But if you find a system that works better, feel free to use it!

Making postulates, saying affirmations, manifesting, synchronicity, and gratitude all work together. They are steps in the same process and, together, they point you in the correct direction and help bring into fruition your goals and desires.

In much the same way that what you focus or concentrate on tends to expand, so does what you are grateful for and what you appreciate.

So ask for what you want to manifest and let the powers that be decide how to give it to you. You don't have to figure out how it will happen. That is not your job. Your job is just to ask and then to express gratitude, even before your desires have come into your life. Accept that they are already there and, lo and behold, they will be!

I didn't always connect the importance of gratitude to the whole process. I know I heard Oprah say years ago that she wrote down things for which she was grateful and she received more abundance. But after listening to many of the New Age philosophers, I have realized that gratitude is so very important. It completes the circle and, without it, there is really no closure and your desired abundance can be hit or miss. So always make gratitude one of your main priorities. You will never regret doing so.

21

Be Careful What You Wish For

My ability to manifest things or make postulates that come true sometimes doesn't work out exactly like I think it will. You do have to be careful how you state what you want to happen. I found out the hard way a few years ago.

In 1992, my mother died from a heart procedure. My father was distraught and he cried for a week. I thought it would do him good to go visit his sister near Asheville for a few days, so I took him, had a nice late afternoon lunch with my aunt and uncle and drove back to my home at that time in Charlotte.

As I was walking in the front door, my phone rang. It was my uncle. "Nancy, we are going to follow the ambulance into Asheville. Your father has had a stroke."

I jumped back in the car and headed back to Asheville. When I got to the hospital, my father was mostly unresponsive. He remained that way for several days and gradually improved to the point that he could communicate with us. But he was paralyzed on one side and was wheelchair bound.

He ended up being in a rehabilitation center for almost a year and then we took him home to Charlotte. He was not happy there. He went to a day care center so he had something to do during the day while my young daughter went to school and I worked. He wanted to go home, which was his house in the North Carolina mountains. So, in 1994, we moved back to the mountains.

The life in Charlotte was difficult because I could not get out of the house except for the time my father was at the day care center. He could not be left alone. The life in the mountains was even more difficult because I did not have the resources I had in Charlotte. I did not have the nurse who came by in Charlotte to bathe my father and check him every day. I didn't have anyone to come in and stay with him while I ran errands.

Finally, I did get him to go to the local senior center a couple of times a week. But I had left my business in Charlotte and I was trying to work at that from a distance and also working another part-time job to make ends meet. After four years of taking care of my father non-stop, I was exhausted. I never seemed to get enough sleep. I kept listening during the night in case he woke up and needed to go to the bathroom. And I had a small child. My husband and I had divorced and he remained in Charlotte when we moved to the mountains, so there really was no help.

One day, I got a call from the senior center. My father apparently had swallowed a prune pit and they were taking him to the local hospital to check him out. I met the ambulance at the hospital. One of our local surgeons, who was an old friend of mine, managed to get the prune pit out and I eventually took my father on home.

That night, my father got very sick. He was running a fever, having chills, and shivering so hard he couldn't remain covered. It scared me that he was suddenly so sick. I called for an ambulance.

As it turned out, when he swallowed the prune pit, he had sucked some fluid into his lungs and he now had pneumonia. He probably would have to remain in the hospital for a week or so, I was told.

That week was a relief to me. I got some sleep, I was able to run my errands without worrying about my father, and I was a good bit less stressed. I went to the hospital to see him every day. During that week, four times I found the bed rail had been left down. My father was paralyzed on one side. If he started to roll out of the bed, there would be nothing he could do to stop himself. I complained to the floor supervisor each time I found the rail down.

Be Careful What You Wish For

After a week, I was told my father would be released the next day and I could take him home.

My first thought was, "Oh no, I'm not ready yet! I am still so tired. I need more time. I am not ready to bring him home and resume my caretaking. I need a miracle."

At four o'clock in the morning, I got a phone call from the hospital telling me my father had fallen out of bed and broken his hip and would be transported to a larger hospital in a nearby town shortly.

I immediately drove down to the hospital, suspecting that someone had left the rail down again. By the time I got there, the rail was up where it should have been. I asked the staff if the rail had been left down and they swore it was up and that my father had apparently climbed over the rail. Well, I'm not accusing anyone of leaving the rail down, but I see no way a paralyzed man could crawl over the rail. But who knows?

So, my father had surgery on the broken hip and he was in the hospital for a couple of weeks. At the end of his time there, the team of doctors told me that my father would need to be placed in a nursing home since he couldn't walk or stand at all. He weighed 180 pounds and I could not begin to lift him. It was his good hip on the non-paralyzed side that he broke. Of course it was.

But he went into a nursing home after that and remained hospitalized until his death a couple of years later.

I felt incredibly guilty for a long time after that. I felt like my thoughts and fervent prayer for help or respite the night before my father broke his hip had set in motion the series of events.

Had I realized there was any possibility of things happening as they did, I would not have even voiced that plea. Maybe I didn't cause anything to happen. Or maybe the man upstairs knew I was at the end of my rope and sent me some help. I don't know. But

I'm more careful with my manifesting these days! And be careful how you state your desire not to leave things open-ended. For instance, if I ask for a new car, I am careful to say something like "my present car is still fine, but I am ready and I now have a new car." This way, I hope, I am making sure nothing bad happens to my old car!

22

The Nature of the Universe

Take a very good look around you. Everything in the room seems very solid and sharply defined, doesn't it? Touch an object near you. Feel its qualities, its hardness or softness, its roughness or smoothness. Look at the walls. Not being Superman, you can't see through them, can you? So you conclude that they are hard, solid objects and that is just the way it is and that conclusion is not open to debate. Right? **Wrong!**

Quantum physicists, who explore the nature of the very small particles that make up every object in our world, have given us a very different version of reality at this level. There are many fine articles and books out now on this subject, but I would like to recommend that you read some of Dr. Deepak Chopra's books or listen to his tapes for an extremely good discussion of the nature of the "real world." Dr. Chopra is an endocrinologist who has combined the best of Eastern mysticism with the best of Western medicine and has become a leading lecturer in the self-help field. While I don't pretend to have the grasp of the concept that he does, I do want to briefly talk about the nature of the universe as many scientists are now viewing it.

Let us begin on an easily understood level. Hold a book in your hands. Feel the hardness of the cover and spine. Press lightly with your fingers. It feels solid. Look closely and you will see no holes in the back, only a solid square of material. Run your fingers across the surface and you will feel only a solid mass with no spaces. However, even when you were in school no matter how long ago, you were taught that every solid object was made up of molecules with spaces between them.

Actually, most of us were taught that the atom was the smallest particle and, when I was in school, splitting the atom was a really big topic of discussion. In the years since, the discovery of various sub-atomic particles has generated whole new fields of study and the information being compiled in these fields is mind-boggling on one hand and totally fascinating on the other.

Now imagine yourself shrinking, shrinking, shrinking, down until you are standing on the book. Things will look quite different to you from this prospective. The grain of the fabric or paper is much more evident now. But there are still no spaces to be seen. So shrink smaller until the fibers in the back of the book are bigger than you are and you can now see spaces between the fibers. If you get smaller and smaller, you will see that the fibers are made up of small particles and then even smaller particles with more and more space between them.

Eventually, if you could keep shrinking, you would finally reach a point where all material, as you know it, would disappear. You would be among the quarks, neutrinos, and all the other particles that make up the playground of quantum physicists. Strangely, when you examined each of these particles, you would find no matter. **Yes, no matter at all!** You would find only incredibly tiny bursts of energy separated by enormous stretches of empty space.

Think of it. Only energy. This energy is pulsating and vibrating. And stranger than that is the fact that *everything in the universe is made up of only vibrating energy on a quantum level*! There is nothing solid. There is only space punctuated occasionally by bursts of energy! So the reality you see around you does not really exist except in your own mind. **You** are the one who perceives this quivering, pulsating, changing mass of energy as the solid room around you and the solid book in your hand. In reality, actual reality, you are holding only pulsating bursts of energy surrounded by vast areas of empty space. That is really hard to imagine, isn't it?

Since everything around you is made up of vibrating energy, does that mean human beings are also made up of only energy? Of course it does, certainly in a literal sense. However, there are New Age teachers who contend that there are different vibratory levels for various states of mind and that one can raise or lower one's vibratory levels by various means such as drinking more water, meditating, exercising, doing random acts of kindness, appreciating beauty, and being grateful. They also teach that lower vibrations are associated with negative emotions and poor health, whereas the higher the vibration, the lighter and healthier the body feels and the more energy and power the person has.

But how is it that many vibrating bursts of energy appear to be your universe? It seems that not only is beauty in the eye of the beholder, actually **everything** is in the eye of the beholder. One can theorize that, since all reality is based solely on being *perceived*, we are creating our own world. Some philosophers have long held that view of the world. Can that be true?

23
Lucid Dreams

I realize that to go from holding a book in our hands to creating our own universe is much too steep a gradient for most of us. In fact, when I was wrestling with this concept, I went outside and looked around me. I looked at the many leaves on the trees and the various colors and shapes of pebbles on the ground. I looked at the colors of nature and the sounds around me. And, you know, I saw absolutely no way I could have even imagined all these things, much less created them! So I concluded that the universe had to be the way I had always imagined it and not as the various New Age philosophers conceived of it. Then, one night, I had a dream that changed everything.

Have you ever had a **lucid dream**? Lucid dreams are those dreams in which the dreamer is aware that he is dreaming and, in many cases, can control what happens. Some people never have lucid dreams or, at any rate, they don't remember them. There are a few people who have lucid dreams quite often and may use these dreams to work out problems or to expand their levels of consciousness. Most of us have these dreams only occasionally. We usually remember them as feeling more real to us and as very special dreams from which we were reluctant to awaken. Many times, the feelings generated during a lucid dream will stay with us the rest of the day and can seem as real as the world around us. These feelings fade slowly as we reluctantly immerse ourselves again in our day-to-day living.

It was just this sort of lucid dream that changed my mind about my abilities to create the things I see around me. I had been doing a lot of reading in metaphysics and I was questioning much about life and the mind's abilities. I think the mind can answer many of these questions if we just allow ourselves to hear. I see the strange, wonderful dream I had as one of these answers.

In my dream, suddenly I was flying. I was flying very low over a coastline similar to the one just off Morehead City and Atlantic Beach in North Carolina. I came to an island sort of like one in the chain that makes up the Outer Banks. I swooped low and came in for a landing on this beach. I didn't have wings or any other visible means of flight. It was merely an ability I took for granted as if I had always been able to fly.

About this time, I realized I was dreaming! It was an earth-shaking cognition! And it didn't take me long after that to also realize that I could control the dream. I became excited even in the dream state because I saw a unique opportunity to test my ability to create with my mind.

I reasoned that it was obvious that I was creating my dream with my mind. Right? There was no other place for the dream to come from except from my own creativity. Therefore, I could see just how complicated a universe I could create in my dream. I stood on the sandy beach in my dream and squatted down so I could examine the grains of sand. They were infinite! There were so many colors, shapes, and sizes. They looked much too complicated for me to be creating them, but there was no other possibility. I looked at each small grain, saw the coloring unique to each one, and marveled to think that it was all in my mind!

So I turned my attention to the trees just beyond the beach and again I saw a scene that looked far too complicated to be in my head. Each individual leaf was totally real looking, complete with veins and cells. The trees had millions of leaves on them! And each one I looked at closely was perfectly formed, just as in the waking world.

By now, even in my dream, I was beginning to realize what a breakthrough I had just made in answering some of my own questions about the nature of existence and my own power to create (and therefore change) it. So I decided to explore further while I had the opportunity.

I suddenly found myself inside a cabin. I was examining the sparse furnishings when the wood grain patterns on the door and the walls caught my eye. They were made up of many subtle shadings of color and the patterns swirled and flowed *just exactly like they do in reality*. There was no possible way I could imagine these complicated patterns—but, without a doubt, I was!

I stood there and touched the door, marveling at the feel of the small ridges in the wood. It felt real and solid. I pushed at the wood and it resisted my hand's pressure just as wood does when we are awake. Now there was no doubt. I could create things with the power of my own mind. At this point, I got so excited that I awakened myself and lost the opportunity to continue my fascinating observations. But it was enough. Yes, it certainly was enough to make me rethink my conclusions about the nature of life and the universe.

Dr. Deepak Chopra describes us as existing in a primordial soup of sorts, an unformed field where all possibilities co-exist and where we choose what we see. I'll be the first to admit that I get lost quickly when I try to imagine this scenario. I get lost even more rapidly when I grapple with Dr. Stephen Hawkings' theory that there are many worlds existing simultaneously—a world for each possibility that could happen. But, among the theoretical physicists, these theories don't seem particularly far-fetched at all!

How do you have lucid dreams? Well, I am certainly no expert, but I have found out some things about dreams and dreaming in my personal life that may point the way. There are a number of books on the subject. I have found that I dream at least some of the time most nights. I think most of us also do. The problem is that we don't remember the dreams. Usually we awaken with a sense that we have been somewhere else, but with no idea of what transpired. Lots of mornings we remember absolutely nothing of any dreams we may have had during the night.

Sometimes I awaken abruptly at a noise or other disturbance and remember that I was in the middle of a dream. I did that this very morning. So if I am in the middle of a dream when I awaken, it is easier to remember it.

I have also found that there is some strange thing with body position, maybe body memory or some such. Before I get up, I lie there for a few minutes and try to remember any dreams I might have had. If nothing pops into my mind, I change my position, turn on the other side, etc., and see if anything is triggered. Strange as this technique sounds, it often works for me. If I get on up and go about my life, any dreams I might have had are lost forever.

Another possible help is to tell yourself you will remember your dreams before you go to sleep. Do this every night. It probably won't work at first. It didn't for me. But if you keep doing it, you will find that remembering your dreams gets easier the more you practice.

Additionally, keep a dream journal. I know you can lie there first thing upon waking and go over your dreams in your head. You may think that you couldn't possibly forget. But they tend to fade away during the day until you can remember only parts. Keep pen and paper on your nightstand beside your bed and write the dream or dreams down before you get out of bed or even change positions. You will find if you read your journal months or years later, that you have absolutely no memory of some of your dreams.

Over the years when I have read about dreaming and various authors' thoughts on dreaming, I remember learning that it usually takes about two weeks for incidents in our real world to make their way into our dreams. I don't think that is the case, but I do think our dreams are symbols of what is going on in our minds. How all these things are interpreted is something I'll leave to others more knowledgeable than I am on this subject! But I will tell you briefly that the dream I had this morning reinforced my belief that it does not take two weeks for things to appear in your dreams.

Yesterday, a friend called from Florida. She invited me to come visit and then told me another of our friends had just come to visit her and they had spent much of their visit going around to various antique stores. In my dream, the same night, I found myself visiting my friend in Florida and we visited a large antique store! That transition took only several hours!

My husband Bruce has always maintained that only the dreamer can truly and accurately interpret his dreams because symbols in the dreams have a different meaning for every person. Dreams are very personal. Although some of our most illustrious psychologists and psychiatrists have claimed there are universal meanings to some of these symbols or, as Carl Jung called them, archetypes, I will have to agree with Bruce's assessment.

If you keep encouraging your dreaming and your remembering of them, you will probably find that a lucid dream or two will occur and then you can discover for yourself how much of a world you can create with your imagination. We are truly remarkable beings with all sorts of amazing powers! And I'm not willing at this point to completely rule out the possibility that we are creating our universe!

24

Miracle in a Snowstorm

As I was driving down a very steep hill near my home recently, I was reminded of an experience I had on that hill during a snowstorm. Was it a miracle? It was to me!

My miracle took place on a snowy night several years ago. It was our first real snowstorm of the winter. I was supposed to go to a meeting at a nearby college, but it was snowing and had been for several hours. When I left my office, I debated about going to the meeting. When my car slid as I left the parking lot, going to the meeting seemed a lot less important. When I slid again at the traffic light at the corner, I decided to turn left instead of right and go on home.

I still had a good bit of tread left on my tires, at least for the flatlands. For mountain traveling in the snow, they just weren't good enough. I was all over the road trying to get to home. I finally pulled off and called my husband Bruce in Tennessee. I don't know what good I thought that would do except give me some moral support and let someone know I was out in the mess and in some trouble.

After talking with him for a few minutes and getting my courage up again, I pulled back on the road only to find I was sliding even worse. So I got halfway home and pulled off the road again.

I called my receptionist who, bless her, offered to come get me and take me home. She said she had not slid on the way home. I told her no, not to get back out in the storm, and wondered why my AWD vehicle hadn't performed as well as hers. After all, my Aviator and her Explorer were both Ford products. Must be the tires, I thought again and pulled out to see if things had changed. They hadn't. This time I made it to the top of the worst hill I had to traverse on my way home, the hill I had been dreading ever since I left the office. I pulled off in a driveway there and spent about 30 minutes trying to get up my nerve to go down the steep hill. I knew that, once I started down, I was committed. There was no way I would be able to stop.

Now that hill, with its steep drop-offs, has always scared me. I remember that it scared my mother when I was growing up and riding with her to my high school where she taught.

Frankly, no matter which way I leave my house in a snowstorm, there is not a safe way. All three of the roads leading away from my house are all formidable in a snow or ice storm with steep hills on all three of them.

Anyway, I finally got my nerve up and pulled out. The snow was swirling and it was about 7:00 p.m., so it was very dark. There is a steep drop-off on the right side of the hill going down. I was terrified of sliding off that side and crashing all the way down the hill because there is no guardrail and there are no trees close to the road to stop a sliding vehicle.

No trees, did I say? As I drove down the steep incline, my heart in my throat, I cautiously looked over toward that steep bank and saw—TREES! Lots of them. Everywhere. Especially, close to the road. I was amazed. Instead of the bank with the endless drop, there were trees close to the road all the way down. I felt safe with those trees close around me seeming to protect me from the possibility of sliding off the road and down the treacherous bank.

As I neared the bottom of the hill without a slip at all, I marveled that there were trees now growing where I thought there were none and how safe they had made me feel. I wondered how I had missed seeing that trees were now growing so near the road. The next morning when I drove up the hill on my way to work, I found out how.

Miracle in a Snowstorm

THERE WERE NO TREES!

My story is a true one. I cannot explain it. While I was driving down that awful hill, I just thought I had not really checked the hill in a couple of years and some trees had grown up without my noticing them. That was absolutely not the case. The trees that I saw were snow-covered and closely spaced and not too far from the road. I have absolutely no explanation for the trees except that someone up above was looking out for me and sent the illusion of trees to give me comfort and courage and I am very grateful.

25

Random Synchronicities

The following incidents are some examples of random synchronicity, or miracles, or guidance from God, or whatever you choose to call them. They are all true. They may just be coincidences or chance happenings, but I don't really believe that. You can judge for yourself. And, when you have finished reading my stories, stop and write down any similar incidents that have occurred in your own life. If you need a convenient place in which to record your own collection of miracles and dreams, etc., look for *The Magic Within Journal*, a companion book to this one, available online from Amazon or wherever you purchased this book. You may be surprised at the number. I keep remembering other examples that I had forgotten.

ೀ I had spent a number of months in Italy back in the '70s and I was headed back to the United States. I decided to see as many countries as I could on my way home.

I flew from Milan to Paris and spent a few days there, walking around the "city of light" and visiting the *Louvre* and the other incredible and marvelous museums. I had such a good time in Paris, not the least of which was eating an American-style fast food meal that I had not seen since I left the States!

I climbed the Eiffel Tower. Yes, I really did! I was completely winded by the time I reached the top. There was a concert taking place in the space under the tower by an orchestra that I think was called the Band of Holland. I sat on a bench nearby listening and enjoying the sunshine. Suddenly, I was struck by the thought that I was lost. I had absolutely no idea how to get back to my hotel on the *Champs-Élysées*. I had been walking around Paris all day. I had covered the Left Bank and I was truly worn out! It was not long before the absurdity of my plight bent me over with laughter. I was sitting at the Eiffel Tower. **Everybody in the world knows where the Eiffel Tower is!**

That realization helped a lot. Since I wasn't "lost" anymore, I merely flagged down a taxi and had the driver take me to the Élysées Palace Hotel where I was staying!

My room was elegant with a nice bar and tall French (of course) doors to a small balcony. I fixed myself a drink and took it out to sit on my balcony and gaze at the beautiful city that I had wanted to visit all through my six years of French lessons in high school and college.

After a few minutes, I realized that there were people sitting and talking on the balcony beside mine. As they continued their conversation, I realized they were speaking English—American English.

I said hello and asked where home was for them. The United States, they told me. I told them I was also American and from North Carolina.

"We are from Raleigh ourselves," they said.

"My brother lives in Raleigh and I lived there myself for more than five years."

They asked me who my brother was and, when I told them his name, they sat there in stunned silence. Finally, they said, "He is our next-door neighbor!"

In a city I had never visited before, thousands of miles from home, what are the odds that the balcony next to mine would belong to my brother's next-door neighbor? We would not have known about each other if we both had not been out on our balconies at that exact time.

꩜ Back in the '60s, when I was in college in the eastern part of North Carolina, I started dating a fellow student who was from Charlotte. Eventually, we became engaged. I made the trip to Charlotte with my fiancé several times and I met his kind and lovely parents. I wanted to have my parents, who lived in the mountains of western North Carolina, meet his parents, but there never seemed to be an appropriate time to get the two sets of parents together.

One weekend, I learned from my parents, there was to be a Shriners Ladies' Night with dinner and a dance at the Oasis Temple in Charlotte. My father was a Shriner and a member of Oasis Temple and he and my mother were planning to drive to Charlotte to attend the event. My fiancé told me that his father was also a Shriner and he was sure his parents would attend the same event. We told both sets of parents to be on the lookout for each other.

On the night of the Shrine event, the Temple was quite crowded. There were many hundreds of attendees at Ladies' Night and my parents despaired of ever finding my fiancé's parents in the huge crowd. They were standing in line waiting to be seated and served.

There was an announcement over the loudspeaker asking each couple to introduce themselves to the people next to them in line. Yes, I'm sure you have guessed it! My parents turned around and found they were introducing themselves to my fiancé's parents! Again, there were huge odds. The two couples sat together for the evening and got well acquainted.

꩜ And then there are the chance occurrences. I went down to Cocoa Beach for the funeral of my favorite aunt. Several of us drove to the Cocoa Beach Pier and proceeded to walk on the beach. As we were heading back to the parking lot, I heard someone yell, "Nancy!"

I looked around and found my daughter's seventh-grade teacher and his wife waving at me. They were staying in Florida for a while not far from the pier and had come out for a walk also. Chance meetings like this are a little more commonplace, but still have a bit of magic attached!

∽ Have you ever noticed how you sometimes get answers in totally unexpected ways from off-the-wall sources?

In the '50s, I went to a private girls' camp near Asheville. I stayed all summer and really enjoyed my time there. My fellow campers were fun and, the girls in my cabin were especially fun. I had a great summer. One thing that made my summer so much fun, besides the fact that I learned to swim, was that my counselor was wonderful. She was a college senior and was there for all of us. I'm sure we made her life miserable occasionally when her boyfriend visited and we peeped out at them from behind trees and, generally, gave them little to no privacy! Her name was Judy Brown and we all adored her.

Through the years, I tried to find someone who knew where Judy had come from and where she had gone after her time with us. My uncle was even vice president of the whole college and resort association with which the camp was associated and when he tried years later, he couldn't learn anything about what had happened to my beloved counselor.

Many years later, after college, I worked as a social worker in the eastern part of the state. In the agency, there was an older woman, a longtime employee, who was in the last stages of cancer, but who bravely kept coming to work whenever she felt okay.

One day I was talking with her and she mentioned that her son and daughter-in-law were coming to spend the weekend with her and she was so looking forward to the visit.

I cannot remember how the subject came up exactly. I think she was telling me about her son and his job. Then she talked about his wife, Judy, who was so delightful. I still didn't think much about what she was saying until she told me that her son and his wife had met in college and he had even traveled to see her several times during the summer when she was a counselor at this camp in the mountains and she named my camp.

"When was that?" I asked, trying not to get my hopes up. "And what was her last name?"

"It was sometime in the mid-fifties," she said. "Her name was Judy Brown."

Wow! After some questioning, it was obvious that her daughter-in-law was truly my Judy Brown! That weekend, she gave Judy my number and we were able to catch up almost twenty years later.

It was only a couple of months later that my friend at DSS succumbed to the terminal illness. She was able to connect me with Judy during the only possible window that existed.

I was very upset when my mother died from a heart catheterization. It was unexpected and I was not prepared for such a thing to happen. She died in the hospital in Charlotte and, the next day, my father, my daughter, and I headed to the mountains where my parents lived to prepare for the funeral.

I was morose, terribly depressed. My mother was not just my mother; she was also my best friend. We planned the ceremony and got everything lined up. I was okay as long as I was busy. But I got all the arrangements done and found myself at loose ends.

I went outside and walked around the house. It was near the end of September and, although it was sunny, the air had the crisp chill of fall. I leaned against the north side of the house and talked aloud to my mother.

"I just need to know that you are okay. Can you send me some kind of sign to let me know you are all right?"

Suddenly, the calm of the afternoon was interrupted by a breeze that blew around the corner of the house and parted the six-inch-tall grass directly in front of me. There, heretofore hidden, was a perfect purple violet blossom nestled in the grass.

Violets don't bloom near the end of September in the mountains. They bloom at that location in April and May and are long gone by late summer. And there was another important fact: violets were my mother's favorite flower. In April and May, she always picked them and put them into a little glass hat vase for our table.

○∾ When I got engaged, my fiancé gave me a very nice ring with a pear-shaped emerald surrounded by diamonds. The ring had come from a longtime friend of his named Paul, who was a jewelry wholesaler supplying local Charlotte jewelry stores. The ring needed to be made a bit smaller. Paul cautioned me to have it done at a reliable jeweler and gave me the name and address of a friend of his who performed such services.

At my first opportunity, I took my new ring to this establishment to get it sized. When I walked in, I thought the man who ran the shop looked vaguely familiar. He looked like Omar Sharif. I actually knew a man who looked like that when I was growing up in the North Carolina mountains, but I had not seen this person in nearly thirty years and I had no idea what had ever happened to him.

We measured the ring and made all the arrangements. The man was filling out the ticket and I gave him my name. He snapped his head up and took a very close look at me.

"You aren't Odes Stroupe's daughter, are you?" he asked me.

When I confirmed that I was, he introduced himself and, yes, he was the person out of my distant past who had been married briefly to a member of my extended family.

After my fiancé and I married, we bought a house in Charlotte. At the time, I had become good friends with the wife, Willie, of the jewelry wholesaler Paul. I was redoing the house and was putting up some vinyl wallpaper. Willie, who had just put up some vinyl wallpaper in her house, offered to come help me.

When she arrived at my house, she was stunned at the location. She had lived next door when she was a child and her best friend had lived in my house. She knew the history of the house and told me about a small fire that damaged part of the basement and the subsequent remodeling that took place afterwards. (I didn't even know there had been a fire and never would have known without Willie's input, although the evidence was there in the rafters in the basement if you knew where to look!)

Sometimes even the small things are incredible coincidences. I grew up in a small town in the western North Carolina mountains. We had many summer visitors, some of whom even had summer houses in our area and lived in Florida most of the year. There were several members of one of our prominent families who traveled back and forth in such fashion.

One summer when one of these families came for the summer months, they brought a friend of their daughter's with them. I was surprised to find that this friend was a former cabin-mate of mine at a summer camp we had both attended some years before.

I never met the daughter of another couple who were in this same family. The parents came several times to visit and they kept telling me they had a daughter who was my age that they would like me to meet. However, each time they came from Florida to visit, she remained in Florida with friends.

Several years later, when I went off to college in the eastern part of the state, I accepted a date with a guy who was in one of my classes. His roommate had a blind date with a girl he had never met and my date had agreed to double date so the situation wouldn't be so awkward. Safety in numbers, I guess!

Anyway, the other guy's blind date turned out to be another freshman like I was and, wonder of wonders, she was the daughter of the couple who had visited my hometown and expressed their wish that I meet their daughter! You just can't make up this stuff, can you? (Actually, I guess I could, but this story is true!)

The world seems to be getting smaller and smaller. Several years ago, I was in Greeneville, TN, and my husband Bruce and I stopped at Waffle House for breakfast. On our way in, I noticed a motorcycle parked near the entrance that had a large orange head sticking out of a backpack behind the seat. Curious, I just had to check it out. Laughing, I called to Bruce to come see the "head." It was wonderful, a goofy caricature of a face under that shock of orange hair. I was still laughing when we went in and someone yelled, "Nancy!"

The woman, dressed in black, was familiar and so was her companion who was at the cash register paying their bill. But you know how sometimes when you see someone in a totally unfamiliar setting, it takes a minute to place him? I kept thinking I knew these people—and then I got it! Fay and Larry Woodie.

The Woodies drove for our newspaper for several months until they stopped so they could take a job driving a truck. We really missed them. They were so helpful and friendly. No matter that winter threw out some really bad stuff, Fay and Larry handled it and got those papers delivered—with a smile and very good humor, too!

It turned out the motorcycle, and the head, belonged to the Woodies.

"It's Larry's sister," Fay joked. She quickly added, "I'm not actually that mean. Larry doesn't have a sister!"

The Woodies always delivered the paper together. They are working their present job together.

"We don't want to be separated," Larry said. "That's what I told them when we took the trucking job."

In a day and age when people are going every which way, that's nice. And it was nice to see them and catch up. What are the odds? Had we been a few minutes later, we would never have seen them. What are the chances I would know the owners of the motorcycle with the orange head? Greeneville is two hours away from Newland. Fay told me that she and Larry love Davy Crockett Park near Greeneville and they come over occasionally.

Sometimes there are strange occurrences, but they don't fit easily into any category. For instance, both of my daughter's grandmothers died on the same day two years apart. And, in the intervening year, as it was my aunt's 90th birthday, we had a big party. I know this is a minor and possibly meaningless coincidence, but what are the chances that both grandmothers would die on the same date?

26

More Small Miracles

The summer after I finished the fourth grade, I went off to Camp Montreat for Girls near in the small resort town of Montreat (famous as the place where evangelist Dr. Billy Graham lived) near Asheville, NC. Although the camp itself was on one side of the town, the camp stables and riding rings were on the east side near the gates that have always marked the entrance to the town. We campers were transported to the stables by bus and we usually went three days per week to take our riding lessons.

The horses apparently were brought up from the Clardy Farms near Ocala, FL, and the Clardy girls, Jane and her sister, taught us English equestrianship. Those were lessons I really enjoyed and the setting there on the side of the mountain was beautiful. I also enjoyed how we could roll over and over down the long, grassy slope as we waited for the bus to take us back to camp.

I had an uncle, Dr. Ivan Stafford, who was a vice-president (usually in charge of development and fundraising) at various colleges over the years. He came back to the western North Carolina area when he was offered the vice president's position at Montreat-Anderson College in Montreat. My family was excited that Uncle Ivan and Aunt Melba were moving back. They had been in Charleston, WV, where my uncle had been vice-president of Morris-Harvey College (now the University of West Virginia at Charleston).

After renting a house for a year or two in Montreat, the Staffords bought land and began building their own house. I was amazed when they took me to see their new house site. Their house was being built on the very space where the old Camp Montreat stables and riding rings had been! And the whole slope I had spent so many hours rolling down while waiting for the bus was their new front yard! I could not believe my eyes!

My next true story also includes my Uncle Ivan. The Staffords had built their Montreat house my senior year in high school. I was getting ready to go off to college the next fall and I had not decided which school to attend. I had applied and been accepted at Wake Forest, UNC Women's College (now UNC-Greensboro), and UNC-Chapel Hill.

It was a difficult decision. My father, in what I thought was a very unlikely move, told me that I probably didn't want to go to Wake Forest because "those Baptists probably won't let you dance and have a good time!" As he had always been extremely strict, it was unusual to hear such words from him!

My uncle knew the presidents of all three schools and he arranged to take my mother and me around the state to meet all these presidents and let them show me around! I'll bet there are not many people who have chosen their college in such a manner!

It was a very interesting day with lots of travel, lots of tours, and lots of shaking hands! I liked all three presidents and all three campuses.

Then my uncle threw us a curve ball. Since we were covering the state, he had one more president and one more school he wanted to visit. This school was not on my list. In fact, it was a new school that had just opened in Scotland County, a Presbyterian school called St. Andrews Presbyterian College, named after the patron saint of Scotland. His friend, college president Dr. Ansley Moore, had a summer house in Montreat and Uncle Ivan knew him well. Dr. Moore had recently had a heart attack and my uncle wanted to see how he was doing. So we went to Laurinburg for our fourth visit of the day.

While we were in Laurinburg, we were given a tour of the brand new college campus. It was beautiful! There was a big lake in the middle of the campus. The dorms and athletic facilities were on one side and the academic facilities were on the other. There was a long causewalk that connected the two sides. All along the causewalk were flowering trees and flowers. It was heavenly. The buildings and the dorms were new. The dining room had by-the-lake dining and some of the classrooms fronted on the other side of the lake. It was a place of peace. I fell in love.

And there, in the middle of the campus, my uncle saw a familiar face. The student who happened to walk by us stopped, did a double take, and said, "Dr. Stafford!"

It turned out he was the son of one of my uncle's Morris-Harvey board members back in West Virginia and he was a junior at St. Andrews and was the student body president for the next year. He stopped everything he was doing and showed us around. I was so impressed that I went home and immediately applied to St. Andrews.

I spent the next four years of my life there and, upon arrival, I again ran into my uncle's friend who was the student body president. His name was Ted and he made sure I knew where everything was and introduced me to a lot of people who included me in various activities.

A chance desire on my uncle's part to extend our trip and see his old friend changed my entire life, both then and in the many years that followed. I worked in Laurinburg for two years after I got out of school and then worked for another two at the mental health center and inpatient unit in nearby Lumberton.

While I am talking about my wonderful Uncle Ivan, I must tell you a couple of stories about him—nothing miraculous, but interesting enough.

The house he built on the old camp stable grounds was one level down from world famous evangelist Dr. Billy Graham. The Grahams and the Staffords were friends and often exchanged vegetables from their gardens. My Aunt Melba taught the Graham kids in high school.

Uncle Ivan often was asked to deliver sermons at the local churches and, sometimes, he would find Billy in his audience, taking notes. Afterwards, Billy would ask Ivan for permission to use some points from his sermon, which always flattered my uncle. Of course, I admired Uncle Ivan for delivering his sermon and keeping his composure knowing Billy Graham was in his audience!

Also, Uncle Ivan was famous for spotting a church out in the country having dinner on the grounds and stopping to offer a blessing in return for a meal! (He never went home hungry!)

Another rather strange thing about Ivan and Melba Stafford—after a marriage that endured and thrived for 59 years, they died on a Monday afternoon around 4:00 p.m. EXACTLY ONE WEEK APART!

༄ My stepson, Bub, met his future wife, Tracy, in school in Raleigh. After dating for a couple of years, they decided to get married. As she was from the Raleigh/Knightdale area, the ceremony and the surrounding events were to be held there.

There was a rather large rehearsal dinner in a local restaurant held as part of the celebratory events. My husband, my daughter, and I were seated at a big table with Tracy's relatives. Her grandmother, Doris, was a lovely person and we enjoyed meeting her and talking with her.

After making a lot of small talk, I learned that Doris had lived in New Bern for years, but had moved back to the Raleigh area. We were from Charlotte at the time, but I had a brother who was a lawyer in Raleigh in a prominent law firm. I asked Doris if she had ever met my brother Odes.

"Oh my gosh," she exclaimed, "of course I know him and his wife, Lillian." And then she said, "I also know your parents. They came to our house in New Bern."

No way! That just couldn't be, I thought. How could this woman I had never met before know my mother and father?

So we figured it out. The synchronicity was just amazing!

My brother's wife, Lillian, had a father named Edwin. By pure coincidence, or synchronicity, Edwin's very best friend in the world, Jack Taylor from New Bern, just happened to have been married to Tracy's grandmother Doris! (By this time, Jack had passed away.)

I knew Lillian's parents very well. I visited with Edwin and Fannie when I occasionally went to Raleigh from the mountains. For years, I had heard tales of Jack Taylor and the escapades he and Edwin got into, including getting shot by Indians on one of their trips out west (I'm serious!).

I remembered that my parents had gone to Morehead City and Atlantic Beach one summer with my brother and his wife and had met Jack and his wife (who turned out to be Doris). Then they had stopped by the Taylor house in New Bern on their way back home to the North Carolina mountains. So, yes, Doris did know my parents!

In talking with Tracy to remember just how all this interaction took place, I found there was a little more to the story. My daughter's first cousin, Katie, married a doctor who is a Taylor from New Bern. We wondered if there were a connection.

No, Tracy told us, but Katie does teach dance at a New Bern dance studio with another instructor who is also a Taylor and is a cousin of the New Bern Taylors of my story!

The MAGIC Within

❧ I had a close friend who seemed to be happily married. One day, he came by the house and confessed that he and his wife, Janey, had split several months earlier, but that he had been too embarrassed to tell anyone. He said that when friends invited them places, they got together and attended as though they were still together and no one was aware of the real situation. He told me his wife had moved in with one of her girlfriends in a local apartment complex. He thought his wife might have been cheating on him, but he didn't know for sure. And, he said, he didn't know how to find out. He gave me her number at her friend's apartment.

I called his wife on her phone and Janey told me they had separated, that there was no one else, and she was still working for her boss who was an attorney in the area.

That same day, another friend of ours who had installed an alarm system for us came by to check on it. He also worked for the local telephone company. Just on a whim, I asked him if he had any way to check out phone numbers and see where they originated. He said he could and asked me what number I needed to have checked. (I'm not naming any names here, because this practice may have been totally illegal and I don't want to get anyone in trouble. Of course, it has been probably 35 years since then.) I told him the number.

A couple of days later, he called me and said he had checked the number and it was very strange. He said any calls to the number in question were routed to the apartment and were then relayed to a house in a rather exclusive resort development just over the state border in South Carolina. Well, that was interesting and it gave me a place to look further.

I looked up the home address of the attorney for whom the wife worked, and learned that his home was in the same South Carolina resort development. So I got in my car and rode the twenty or so miles to the development. I was very familiar with this housing development. It was an exclusive one with a nice golf course and country club and I had booked the entertainment there with the bands I handled many times. I knew the manager of the club very well.

My first stop was at the clubhouse. The manager told me which house belonged to the attorney, so I drove by there. There was a big FOR SALE sign in the yard with the name of a real estate company.

After I returned home, I called the real estate company. I managed to get a very chatty agent who told me all about the house in which I professed an interest. I also asked if that was the house where this particular attorney lived. The agent told me that it was and that he and his fiancé, Janey, were getting married soon and moving to the beach.

Wow! And my friend had no idea. He still had hopes of getting back together with his wife. I hated to dash his hopes, but it turned out well. He met another lady soon and has lived happily with her ever since. His ex-wife did marry the attorney and they did move to the beach. But I had all the connections to find out easily what was going on for my friend. I found out more through synchronicity and meant-to-be connections in a couple of days than my friend had been able to learn about his own wife in several months! Some things are just meant to be!

Ever had a hunch that you felt so strongly about that you couldn't ignore it? The next two stories started out just that way.

☙ One weekend, my husband's band played at Myrtle Beach at the Dunes Club, a favorite play venue for all of us. The manager, Manny Letts, was a dear friend and we enjoyed the members.

On this weekend after the job, the rest of the band made the four-hour return trip back to Charlotte. Jerry and I had decided to stay until the next day and we were spending the night at the house of an old friend, Jack Price, who had owned a nightclub in Myrtle Beach for years.

We left the Dunes Club with our van and all the band equipment packed up in the 5x8 trailer we were towing. We enjoyed visiting with Jack and then we finally went on to bed. Neither of us could sleep.

"I am worried about our stuff out in the trailer," Jerry said. "I feel like someone might try to break in and steal the equipment."

"I am also feeling uneasy," I replied.

"Let's go sleep in the van," he said. So we did.

At 5:00 a.m., Jack came out to the van and woke us up.

"I just got a call from the Charlotte police," he said. "Your house has been broken into and they are trying to find you."

At that time, there were no cell phones but, thankfully, we had let several people back in Charlotte know where we were. So our anxiety and worry proved to have some foundation, but we identified the wrong target. Our house in Charlotte was robbed instead of our 5x8 trailer with all the equipment.

My main concern with the Charlotte robbery was whether or not my beloved silver Persian, Nikki, was okay. The police relieved my mind. They said he was outside when they answered the call (he never went outside) and, when they opened the door, he shot in so they figured he belonged. We lost some items like a gun, some bows, and other things, but my precious Nikki was okay so I was so happy about that! Needless to say, we made a very quick trip back to Charlotte and my reunion with Nikki was a joyous one!

The next incident is very similar. It also involves a hunch and an attempted robbery.

More Small Miracles

❧ Jerry and I were on an extended trip to New England and Nova Scotia. We decided to stop in Boston and visit the ship, the *Constitution*. Jerry had always wanted to build a model of the famous ship, so we took advantage of our nearness to tour the ship.

We parked in the parking lot near the *Constitution* wharf, locked everything up tight, set the alarm, and took off to visit the ship.

We spent about 20 minutes on board the ship when we both turned to each other at exactly the same time and said, "I have a bad feeling about the van."

Well, that was all it took for us to make a mad dash off the ship and into the parking lot where we had parked our van.

When we got in sight of the van, we saw that both front doors were wide open, so we ran that much faster. There was no one there when we reached the van. I guess they had seen us coming and they took off. Somehow they had circumvented the alarm because it had not gone off. We checked and there was nothing missing, not even the gun we always carried in the van.

We found the security guard for the parking lot and told him what had happened. He told us that robberies took place fairly often in that parking lot and the adjacent lots and that we had been lucky.

So, Jerry stayed with the van, gun in hand, while I went back to the ship and finished my tour. Then, when I returned to the van, I sat there with the gun until Jerry finished his tour of the ship.

I have no idea where the spot-on hunches came from in this true story or the previous one. Information sent from God? Or was it the universe giving us a little nudge? I think this sort of information probably is imparted to us much more often than we realize and, many times, we just don't notice.

27

A Few More Stories

In Chapter 19 of this book, I talked about the odd synchronicities associated with how I met my husband Bruce. There is a bit more to that story.

❧ Bruce's late wife. Julie, who (I'm convinced) had something to do with getting Bruce and me together, also seemingly had her hand in quite a few other things. For several years after her death, feathers would show up everywhere Bruce went. He kept finding feathers—big feathers, little feathers—lots of them. He kept remarking, "I found another one!" I finally asked him what the feathers meant to him. He told me that Julie had a fondness for feathers and considered them to be very lucky. She always saved the feathers she found in unusual places where feathers were not normally found. Bruce felt the feathers he found everywhere he went in the year or two after Julie died were signs from her that she was okay.

Bruce later told me that, especially in the first few weeks after Julie died, the lights in his house would blink on and off as he passed through a room. He always felt it was Julie communicating with him.

When one of Bruce's relatives died, the relative's wife told Bruce that her husband had told her before he died that he had seen Julie, and that she had come to help him make the transition.

But the strangest thing connected with Julie and the feathers is what happened after Bruce had a massive stroke and was hospitalized for several weeks in a Tennessee hospital's stroke center. There were feathers literally EVERYWHERE! There would be feathers swirling around my daughter and me when we went across the parking lot. The ground would be littered with feathers outside the entrance. When we went into Bruce's room, we would find feathers on his bed, on his table, in the sink, and I even found one stuck to the mirror in his bathroom. One time I found a feather on his newly delivered tray of food.

The hospital was not the only place where I found feathers. Almost immediately, the feathers started showing up at our house. I had never noticed anything more than an occasional feather prior to Bruce's stroke. You may not agree, but I tend to think it was Julie letting me know she was watching over her beloved Bruce!

☙ Lights and energy fields seem to be communicating tools in so many cases. It certainly was with my father, as you will see in Chapter 29 (Messages From Beyond). That was also the case with the death of my sister, Joyce.

The evening my sister had a stroke, we had gone to an outdoor music venue in the NC mountains near my home. We had just gotten there when Joyce stumbled, caught herself, and suddenly started stuttering. She couldn't seem to get words out. I immediately suspected she had had a stroke. When I suggested the hospital, Joyce nodded and managed to say, "Yes. Something isn't right."

So we rushed her to the local hospital. They immediately realized Joyce had had a stroke and they had her airlifted to the same stroke center in Tennessee where Bruce went years later. We drove there as fast as we could. The outlook was not good, but we were still hopeful as she had talked with us a little before she was intubated for the helicopter trip to Tennessee. We spent much of the night at the hospital. We were all so tired that Bruce, my daughter, and I finally drove the hour to our Tennessee home to get a few hours' sleep. Joyce's husband, Lon, decided to stay with Joyce.

We got up early the next morning, around six, and my daughter and I were in my bathroom getting ready to go back to the hospital to see about Joyce.

Suddenly, all the lights in the room dimmed, and then got brighter, brighter still, and so bright they hurt our eyes and then returned to normal.

My daughter and I looked at each other and just said, "Oh no, Joyce. Something has happened."

In about five minutes, the phone rang and it was Lon at the hospital. "Joyce just had another massive stroke," he said, "and this time they think she is brain-dead."

That did turn out to be the case. Although the hospital kept Joyce on a ventilator until her children could get there later that day, she was lost to us at the time of the strange light behavior. Since Joyce had been around when my father died and was a witness to what happened to the lights then, I can only believe that it was Joyce telling us goodbye.

A few years ago, I attended a church supper that was held to raise money for a family who needed help. I don't remember exactly why the family was in dire straits, perhaps a house fire or the illness of a family member, but I will never forget what happened that night.

I was helping bring the food out from the kitchen and also helping to serve the plates. We had a huge turnout. We had warmed many trays of rolls, enough to feed an army, we thought. However, about halfway through the meal, we realized we were running out of rolls. We had plenty of everything else. I went through the whole kitchen and looked in every container and bag to see if we truly had used all the rolls or if we had overlooked any somewhere. I also looked in the refrigerator and the ovens. Nope. No rolls. I went into the main dining area to tell the ladies in charge that there were no more rolls. They said they would just tell people the rolls had run out and give them a little more food.

I returned to the kitchen and I saw a red light glowing on the oven where I had looked a few minutes earlier. Funny, I thought, I didn't notice before that the oven was on.

I crossed the kitchen and pulled open the oven door. To my absolute shock, there in the oven were several trays of rolls nicely browned and almost ready to serve! No way! Where on earth had they come from? And who had turned on the oven?

I pulled out the trays of rolls and took them to the dining room to show the ladies in charge. They were also dumbfounded and no one admitted to putting the rolls in the oven. There was now plenty of bread to feed everyone present. I asked everybody who had anything to do with the supper about the rolls. Everybody there denied any knowledge of where the rolls came from or how they ended up in the oven. I thought for a while someone was playing a trick on me although I couldn't figure out how it had been done. I had not left the kitchen for long, the doorway was in my sight the whole time I was gone, there was no one else in the kitchen when I went to the dining area, and no one went into the kitchen while I was gone.

In the years since, I have never figured how the rolls appeared out of nowhere, but I guess if Jesus could make loaves and fishes expand to feed a lot of people, God certainly could give us the needed rolls for our benefit supper!

My daughter had a real miracle happen to her back when she was in high school. It was a miracle for which I was, and still am, very grateful.

She had a babysitting job with a beautiful little five-year-old girl who was the daughter of one of her teachers at the high school. She and the little girl (let's call her Jessie so her parents don't have a heart attack reading this account all these years later!) had been out for a drive in my daughter's car.

The trip was uneventful until they reached the turn for our road. The main highway is a steep hill in the direction from which they were coming and they had a little speed up going down the hill. There was a lot of loose gravel on our road from some pothole patches that had been done recently.

As my daughter made the turn into our road, she applied the brakes and they locked. The car started sliding on the loose gravel and she realized that she also could not turn the steering wheel and the car was heading for the area where the bank dropped off steeply.

She told the child, "Brace yourself. I can't stop!"

The car careened toward the edge of the bank. Suddenly, as the rear wheels touched the foot-wide grass verge at the edge of the road, the car came to an abrupt and complete stop. My daughter and the child sat there, unable to believe the car had stopped and had not gone off the bank.

After a few minutes, my daughter managed to drive on to our house. She came in telling me, "There is a God! He just saved our lives!" She told me what had just happened.

I hopped in my car and drove to the end of the road. Sure enough, there were black skid marks leading from the entrance of our road to the edge of the bank. I got out and looked closely at the skid marks.

The tires had not left marks just in the road. They had left major visible indentions in the grass at the edge of the road. The indentions stopped about four inches from the drop-off! I looked over the bank and saw, to my horror, a tall four-by-four post sticking right up in the exact place to have punched through the car's windshield had the car gone on over the bank.

I stood there for a long time trying to understand what sort of force could let the car tires make such ruts in the grass and then stop the car short before it went over the bank. I couldn't see any way at all. After a few minutes, I got out my camera and took pictures of the skid marks, the ruts, and of the post below the road. Over the years, I have pulled out these pictures a number of times and I have never failed to be astonished and then extremely grateful!

◠◡ Several days ago, one of my very good friends stopped by the house. I was telling Marilyn about the new book, *The Magic Within*, that I was working on and she reminded me of a miracle that happened in her life a few years ago.

Marilyn's late husband, Jerry, always had made a special deal about her birthdays. One year, he gave her a lovely salmon pink rosebush. They planted the rose in the backyard, up on the bank where they could see it when it bloomed. The rose bloomed for a number of years, until Marilyn didn't get a chance to fertilize and care for the rose and, covered in weeds and leaves, it finally stopped blooming.

Every year Marilyn meant to clean up the area around the rosebush and to see if she could encourage the rose to bloom again. But, as with many of us, she never got around to it.

In the meantime, her husband developed cancer and eventually died.

The next year after Jerry's death when Marilyn's birthday rolled around, she was very despondent. Jerry had been the one to make sure she had wonderful birthdays and, although her adult daughters tried to celebrate the day, it just wasn't the same without Jerry.

Marilyn came home that day depressed and really missing Jerry. She walked out her back door and, as she looked around, she noticed a flash of salmon pink up on the bank behind the house. Puzzled, she walked nearer to see what it was.

She was very surprised to find a single, large, perfect salmon pink blossom on the old neglected rosebush that had not bloomed at all in several years. She still is sure that Jerry somehow caused the rose to bloom to tell her happy birthday and to raise her spirits on her special day.

Once upon a time, I was the publisher of a Boone-based magazine entitled *All About Women of the High Country*. In one of our issues, we had featured a wonderful young singer/musician who, we thought, would surely take the country music world by storm. And she was engaged to another wonderful artist who showed just as much talent. The couple would go far, we were sure.

And we were right. This couple is now known as Darin and Brooke Aldridge and, if you know anything about country music, you will immediately recognize their names. Darin and Brooke are very familiar faces on the Grand Ole Opry and Brooke has been named the IBMA female vocalist of the year four times.

I was on my way back to the mountains from Charlotte one weekend and I happened to see that Darin and Brooke were playing a benefit that was being held in a tent near Darin's hometown of Cherryville. It was a very small detour from my usual route home, so I decided I would go by there and say hello and perhaps stay to hear some of their wonderful music.

Soon after I parked in the big field, I spotted Brooke and Darin in one of the tents. I went in to say hello. Oddly enough, although Darin grew up in Cherryville, his father grew up in the High Country and was my neighbor. The third person I saw when I entered the tent was Darin's father, my old neighbor and childhood friend.

A Few More Stories

I suddenly realized there was another familiar face from my past in the tent. My old boss, Rick, from my days working as a therapist at the Charlotte Detox! Just the best boss you could ever have! He helped my husband set up and surprise me with a fully operational darkroom for my birthday one year. I had not seen Rick for many, many years.

When we talked a bit, I found out Rick was managing the Aldridge duo and had been doing so for several years. I had no idea he had any interest in music or that he was a pretty good musician himself. And I certainly was surprised that he was arranging bookings and such for the Aldridges. Also, he was extremely good friends with Darin's dad. I thought Rick had retired from the mental health field and was enjoying retirement in the Charlotte area. I will say that I had thought about Rick often and always had the idea in my mind that I would like to find Rick and catch up!

A similar incident happened a couple of years ago when my daughter and I went to the beach for a quick weekend trip. We were there for a few days only and we tried to cram as many activities into our short time as possible. One of our "must not miss" stops was the Oceanic Restaurant and Pier on Wrightsville Beach, so of course we made time for a nice meal there on Saturday afternoon.

The area was crowded and, knowing how busy the Oceanic Restaurant is around suppertime, we decided to go early around 4:00 p.m. Sure enough, there was a vacant table out on the pier, which we always preferred over eating inside. So we settled in to enjoy a fabulous meal in a wonderful setting.

We thought we were seeing things when a couple of people stopped at our table and exclaimed, "I don't believe this! Nancy and Danica!"

We could not believe Sue and George were standing before us! Sue had been the director of the local chamber of commerce in the mountains when I had been president of that same organization. Then she had moved from the mountains to a town near Rocky Mount in the eastern part of North Carolina. I had not seen Sue and George for a long time.

As for synchronicity, we had been talking about Sue and George and how much we wanted to see them. We had gone to supper a couple of hours earlier than we usually did. We chose Saturday night to go to the Oceanic and we had gone to a couple of our other favorite restaurants on the other nights of our stay. Sue and George had decided to try the Oceanic (they had not been there before) and they also decided to go early to avoid the crowd. They ended up on the pier and not inside because there was a place on the pier and not one inside. And we were sitting at a place they walked by and they happened to notice us!

The next day, we met on the beach for a quick swim and then we went by their Rocky Mount home and had a quick supper with them before we returned to the mountains. How fortuitous was all that?

◌ I almost drowned when I was nine years old. Really. I was off at summer camp in the North Carolina mountains. I was taking beginner's swimming lessons, but I had not yet learned to swim. But I was trying. The site of the lessons was a very cold mountain lake that never warmed up, even in the middle of summer.

On that day, after we finished our lessons, we were allowed to stay a little while and play in the water. A friend and I kept sliding down the "kiddie" slide into shallow water. That activity finally just got too tame for me. I kept eyeing the big slide. I wanted to try that.

So I made my way to the big blue slide. I was careful. I told myself that if the water got too deep, I would turn around and not venture out any farther. The water never got any higher than a little ways above my waist. I never even considered that the water on the other side of the slide might be deeper!

I climbed bravely up the big slide's ladder. I did have some misgivings when I reached the top and looked down. It was a very long way down! But, hey, I was a big girl of nine. I could do it.

So I pushed off and slid down the slide. It was fun going down. Then I hit the water—and kept going down. Instead of the ground that I expected to easily land on, I didn't find the bottom. And I couldn't swim! Oh, no! What do I do?

Well, I finally did hit the bottom with my feet. The surface was a good ways above me. Suddenly a voice in my mind said, push off from the bottom. I did. I broke the surface and took a big gulp of air. But I went right back down before I was able to yell for help and I didn't know how to keep myself on the surface. So I kept going back down, touching the bottom, and pushing myself back up again. One time, I managed to get a small cry for help out. I kept up my struggles for what seemed like a long time.

Suddenly I felt strong arms wrap around me and propel me to the surface. When we reached the surface, I saw that it was my swimming instructor who had seen that I was in trouble and had come to my rescue. You can believe that I learned to swim that summer! I was not going to find myself in that danger again, even if there was someone looking after me and telling me to push off from the bottom!

A similar incident happened when I was in the first grade. After school, I rode home every day with one of my mother's friends who was a teacher at my school. I always walked down the long set of steps to the parking lot and got in the car belonging to my mother's friend and waited for her until she was finished for the day.

This day, I walked down and got into the car. Very soon, it started raining and then the rain started freezing on every surface. I got cold and then I got scared. The teacher was late and I was afraid she wouldn't come.

Then I thought of my Aunt Melba. She taught eighth grade in a nearby building and I knew her room was on the second floor near the outside fire escape because I had seen it when I visited Aunt Melba's room. Of course, I had made the trip to her room together with my aunt. I had no idea how to get to my aunt's room other than to go up the long fire escape. So that is what I did.

I soon realized that the fire escape was covered in ice and more was building up on the steps by the minute. I clung to the side rail and managed to work my way about three-fourths of the way up. And then I got stuck. I slipped a little, caught myself, and was too scared of falling to the concrete below to venture up farther. I just clung there, not knowing what to do. I couldn't go up; I couldn't go down. I prayed.

Suddenly, a few feet above me, the fire escape door was pushed open. The kindly face of tiny Margaret Ollis, my aunt's teacher assistant, looked down at me. She immediately realized the trouble I was in and she very carefully came down several steps until she could grab my arms and pull me to safety. She told me she had looked out the window at the worsening weather and happened to catch sight of me clinging to the fire escape.

Of course I got in trouble for going up the fire escape, but I didn't care by that point. I was safe and that was all that mattered!

෴ Also strange are the stories people sometimes relate as they are dying. I remember the several days before my grandmother died in the early '60s. She was in and out of a coma and every time she woke up, she told us of incredibly beautiful cities she had been visiting. She also told us my long-deceased grandfather was there with her and so were many of her relatives and friends who had already passed on.

When my stepson's grandmother passed away, she kept insisting that her late husband was there beside her to show her the way home. Everyone took great comfort in her words and it certainly made her transition easier for both herself and her loved ones.

༄ I have one last story about Julie, my husband Bruce's late wife. After Bruce's stroke, my daughter and I spent several months in Tennessee closing the business and the house. Clearing the house was a mammoth undertaking because I had much stuff there, Bruce had even more things there, and nobody had ever cleared out or gone through Julie's things. There were several closets filled with her possessions.

My daughter has always been interested in the lifestyles of the 1800s and 1900s. She sometimes has wished she had lived in the times when men were masculine men and women were ladies. She also has maintained that today's feminism has come close to destroying the traditional roles and has turned most men into something less than yesteryear's strong males. In the months preceding Bruce's incident, she said she wanted to know much more about the past two centuries and how the roles of men and women have changed. She did even decry the fact that she couldn't really find out because all the people are deceased!

While clearing out one of the closets, she came upon a treasure trove of very old books. Apparently Julie had collected hundreds of books written mostly between 1800 and 1930. To my daughter, the books were an amazing find. She has spent years pouring over them, gaining the firsthand knowledge of the many authors about life in those centuries and the roles (and how they changed) of the men and women of that time frame. The books were the perfect answers to the questions she posed to the universe! She is now writing her own books with help from these old books and their long-deceased authors who lived during the times that whetted her curiosity.

Coincidence, synchronicity, or the answer to a prayer? Perhaps all three?

◯∾ Sometimes the coincidences are very small and many people would not even notice them. But you will find that the more you put your attention on them, the more often they will happen.

My daughter lost her pen last week. When she looked for it, she couldn't find it. Suddenly she had a very strong hunch about where the pen might be, although she didn't think she had been near that particular location. But the hunch was so strong, she looked anyway. And found her pen exactly where her hunch led her!

Last week I lost a small flashlight I use a lot. I looked and looked for the small red flashlight to no avail. A couple of nights later, I dreamed where the flashlight was lying. When I got up the next morning, I remembered the dream. I sort of laughed at myself because I was seriously—well, maybe half seriously—considering going to look in the location from my dream. In spite of making fun of myself, I went to look.

And, of course, there was my flashlight!

◯∾ Also, this past week, I was in the grocery store and I picked up some chocolate chip cookies. I'd better get some kind of cookies for my daughter, I thought, since I'm getting some for me. So I picked up a pack of sugar cookies for her.

I came home and was in the kitchen putting up the groceries when my daughter came in. She opened the refrigerator door, grabbed a couple of items and remarked, "A sugar cookie would be great right now."

A Few More Stories

She immediately closed the refrigerator door and found me standing there with my mouth open, holding her cookies in my hand! I just held out my hand and gave them to her.

NEVER in all the years of her life has she asked me for cookies. She doesn't even like many kinds of cookies. I was so surprised. And so was she when I handed her the cookies!

28

Unexplainable Connections

One hears many tales about the strange supernatural connections that occasionally occur between identical twins. I always have been fascinated by these stories and wondered if those connections were anything like the strange supernatural connection I had for years with my own mother.

I didn't notice anything unusual when I was growing up. I was close to my mother, but I was also very independent and she encouraged my efforts to fend for myself and control my own life. The first inkling I had that I might have some special connection with my mother came when I went off to college. On several occasions when I called my mother, I got only the first four or five numbers dialed and, suddenly, she was speaking to me! It turned out that she had been dialing my number at the same time and had not completed her dialing, either. This eerie coincidence happened four or five times while I was in college and kept happening after I graduated, got married, and was living and working in the eastern part of the state. Then things got even stranger.

One Saturday afternoon, I was sitting in my living room reading a book when I was overwhelmed by fright. I was consumed by fear. My heart was racing and my breathing was difficult. These awful feelings lasted for about ten minutes and then everything calmed down and my heart and breathing returned to normal. I told my husband what was happening and neither of us could figure out what was going on. It made no sense. There was absolutely no reason for me to be so scared sitting calmly in my own living room.

A couple of hours later, my mother called. She had quite a tale to tell me. She and my father had been out driving and, suddenly, she looked up and saw a car careening out of control into their lane.

Unexplainable Connections

"There was no way he could miss us," she said. "I knew he was going to crash into us."

Aha! Perhaps I had my answer. "What did you feel when you looked up and saw the car coming?" I asked.

"Pure, stark fear," she said. "It scared me to death! He was coming so fast. It took me a few minutes after he hit us and I realized we had survived for me to calm down. It was an awful experience!"

Well, you can judge for yourself. I know what I believe! And subsequent incidents of similar happenings finally convinced me that through some odd psychic means, my mother passed to me her feelings about the oncoming car.

The next time the odd connection happened, I had been out walking my boxer, Amber. She was a large dog for a female, weighing more than 70 pounds. We had been running in a field that had been recently mowed. There were short four- and five-inch stumps left from bushes and thick weeds. I tripped on one of the roots and went flying. I landed pretty hard and, as I had Amber on a leash wrapped around my hand, I ended up being dragged for a few yards until she realized I was no longer running with her. The fall knocked my breath away. I sat there for a couple of minutes trying to recover. Finally, I picked myself up and Amber and I made it back to my house.

When we walked in the front door, my husband was on the phone with my mother. He later told me her first words when he picked up the phone were: "What's wrong with Nancy? What has happened to her?"

Seriously. I got on the phone and reassured her that I had taken a minor fall and, apart from some possibly cracked ribs, I was fine.

A year or two later, my husband and I went to the mountains to house- and dog-sit while my parents spent a couple of weeks in

Hawaii. All was well for most of the time. We visited with old friends and did some sightseeing while we were there.

A couple of days before my parents were scheduled to fly home, I got a bad feeling about my mother. Somehow I knew it was not a major problem, but I positively knew there was a problem. I told my husband that my mother had been hurt, her foot, I thought, but that it was not really serious. After all the incidents between my mother and me, my husband just shook his head. He was no longer surprised.

Several days later, when we picked my folks up at the airport, my mother limped off the plane with a bandaged foot and ankle. It turned out she had cut her foot on a piece of coral while swimming in the ocean and had been advised to go to the emergency room to get the cut cleaned out. Apparently, she was told that coral could keep growing in the body if it wasn't thoroughly cleaned. We checked our times when I got the "message" from her and, allowing for the time difference, it was within a few minutes of her injury.

Several years later, my mother found a lump in her breast. She had a scheduled biopsy and I came home to be with her. She was frightened. She made me promise that no matter what the biopsy showed, nothing drastic would be done while she was under anesthesia. If she needed surgery, it would be scheduled later so she could be prepared. Of course I promised.

During the procedure, the surgeon came to tell me that the lump was malignant and he tried and tried to get me to agree to go ahead and remove the breast while she was still asleep, even though he had told my mother he would not do that. I was very unhappy with him. I refused adamantly. My brother and my father both backed me up.

When my mother woke up, she understandably was upset over the cancer diagnosis. She was very worried about what to do next.

Unexplainable Connections

I stayed as long as I could that afternoon.

That evening, my bandleader husband had a gig to play with his band in Winston Salem. I ran the lights and sound and collected the money. As I sat there on the bandstand that night, I experienced some very strange feelings. Suddenly, I would feel extreme fright and despairing fear. Things would calm down and I would feel okay for a few minutes and then the cycle would repeat. Later that night, I called my mother and learned that she had been groggy all night and had alternated between sleepiness and stark fear worrying about what to do. Apparently I had picked up on all of her mixed feelings.

I really never understood this strange connection with my mother. I used to tell her that she had better not die because I didn't want to feel that kind of connection! And when she did die, I felt nothing at all. Nothing. Just blankness. Perhaps that was the way it was supposed to happen. The connection just suddenly was gone.

But there is more to my story. The rest involves incidents of synchronicity.

The next day after the band job, I was talking to my mother-in-law about my mother's cancer diagnosis and she remembered that a friend of hers had recently had breast cancer surgery at Duke Hospital in Durham and might have some idea who to contact. She said she would call her.

To make what could be a long story a bit shorter, by the time I got back to the mountains the next day, my mother-in-law had called her friend. Her friend had become close friends with the secretary in the office at Duke of one of the country's foremost breast cancer and reconstructive surgeons, so she called her. The secretary called my mother and my mother had an appointment in two days with the great doctor himself for breast surgery and subsequent reconstructive surgery. Wow! That was so easy! Everything, including all the information we needed to make informed decisions, just fell into place. Coincidence? Maybe not.

Over the next six months, my mother had both breasts (yes, there was suspicious tissue in both) removed and with three operations had very successful reconstructive surgery. She also successfully beat the cancer and lived many years after that with no problem at all. She did not even have to do any chemotherapy or radiation.

And, oddly, her doctor from Duke started coming to our area and seeing patients once or twice a month, so she didn't even have to go to Duke for some of her follow-up visits. The doctor and his wife became friends and my mother, who loved to crochet, had given the doctor's wife a number of her crocheted items over the years.

That was many years ago in the late seventies. A couple of years ago, there was a woman from our area who was battling cancer and was being treated by a doctor at Duke. She was staying with friends in Durham while she took some of the necessary treatments.

When the winter weather became treacherous in the mountains, the woman's family worried that she had the wrong car for bad weather in Durham and would be in trouble if she tried to come home for a visit. They decided take a Jeep to her and asked a friend of my daughter's to help arrange the transfer. He asked my daughter to go along.

They made the four-hour trip, found the residence where the woman was staying near Durham, and made the transfer of vehicles. The woman was staying with a very gracious and attractive older lady in a beautiful home. When the lady asked my daughter where she was from, my daughter told her. The lady then said she had once known a wonderful lady from the mountains who was a teacher named Nancy Stroupe and asked my daughter if she had known her.

My daughter, stunned, replied, "She was my grandmother!"

Unexplainable Connections

The lady, who was equally stunned, left the room and returned with all the crocheted items my mother had given to her over the years. Everything was very carefully wrapped and preserved. She said she was the widow of the doctor who had operated on my mother at Duke all those years ago and, over the course of my mother's surgery and reconstruction, they had become acquainted and had grown to be friends.

"I carefully saved these beautiful things," she said. "They were too pretty to use. And now I know why I saved them. Take them and enjoy your grandmother's handiwork!"

What a nice treasure trove from the past! And how unlikely was the chain of coincidences that put them in my daughter's hands?

29

Messages From Beyond

My father's leaving this life took some bizarre twists. The events that transpired before, during, and after his death defy most ordinary explanations and left us with questions no one living can answer.

The last two years of my father's life were spent in a nursing home. For the first year after he broke his "good" hip (the other leg was unusable from a stroke), he was unable to stand and I couldn't lift him. I transferred him to a nursing home that was closer to us for the second year. The staff in that facility encouraged him to try to walk to meals. It worked. Before long, he was able to walk short distances with his walker or a quad cane.

His improvement meant he could go out to dinner occasionally with me, so we tried to do so quite often. I was even hoping he would improve enough that I could finally bring him home.

On one occasion in mid-summer, I took him out to dinner and then brought him to our house so he could visit for a little while. When we got there, he wanted to sit on the deck for a while.

The evening grew a little cooler and it was almost time for me to take my father back to the nursing home. Still, he sat there looking around him at the house, the yard, and the woods.

"What are you doing?" I asked him.

"I'm making memories," he told me. Then he hesitated and said, "If I tell you something, will you promise not to tell anyone else? They would think I was crazy."

I promised and he told me that, for the last month or so, my mother who had died six years earlier had been with him. He said they had long conversations and great visits and she was a great comfort to him at the nursing home. He also told me that when anyone came into his room, he would try to introduce her, but as soon as anyone came in, she disappeared. He was a bit frustrated by her disappearance as he couldn't prove to anyone she was really there, but he seemed to understand that perhaps he was the only one who was supposed to see her.

Then he said something else that really surprised me. He said he didn't think he would be around long. He said he really hated to leave me, and my daughter, but he was going to have to go. He advised me to go ahead and withdraw the money that was left in our joint account so it wouldn't be tied up when he died.

He said he had been hearing a voice whispering in his ear telling him, "You'd better get ready. It's almost time to go."

When I asked him whose voice it was, he said he assumed it was God.

Over the next few days, I had a couple of significant discussions with my father. I had been reading some New Age literature that linked philosophical thought to some aspects of quantum physics and, one writer (I can't remember who) theorized that if spirits or departed souls are energy, perhaps they could communicate by disrupting other energy sources, such as electricity. I talked about this concept at length with my father. We joked about how he could possibly communicate with me by electricity after he was gone. Then he more seriously told me that if it were at all possible to disrupt energy fields when he was in spirit form, he would do so to let me know he was all right. We talked about possibilities being lights and radios.

About a month later, my father was admitted to the hospital. The doctor couldn't tell me exactly what was wrong, but he described it as a "sickness unto death," echoing the title from the famous book written by Danish philosopher Soren Kierkegaard in 1849. In other words, he thought my father was dying, but he could not identify any specific cause. Sure enough, after a week or two in the hospital, my father checked out for good.

An hour or so later, my family was gathered around the dining room table planning all the things we needed to do leading up to the funeral and afterwards. We had been sitting there for about 20 minutes when suddenly the light fixture over the table went out. I knew it hadn't burned out since there were several bulbs in the light, so it had to be that a breaker had tripped. I got a stepstool and climbed up to a cabinet to reset the breaker.

I was thinking why now? Right in the middle of all our planning. And the electrical circuit that included the dining room was one that had never before gone off. I had tripped the one for the kitchen a number of times by vacuuming while running several of the appliances, but never the one in the dining room.

And then it dawned on me! Actually, it dawned on me so hard that I almost fell off the stool! Why now? Of course it was now and it was my father doing exactly what he said he would try to do to let me know he was okay!

I went rushing back into the dining room to tell the rest of the family what I had figured out. And before you say it was a chance occurrence and I am loony, let me tell you that this incident was the start of *literally years* of incidents that centered around my daughter who was about 16 years old when Dad died.

My daughter would walk under a streetlight and it would go out and come back on. It happened many times—literally *hundreds of times*. The radio in her car would go off and come back on.

She tried an experiment one night. She said to her grandfather, "If it is you, please turn on my radio." The radio turned on and no one was in the car. Then she told him to turn it back off. It turned off. She would walk into a restaurant and the lights would go off. Once, she got out of a car in Wilmington, NC and the lights went off all along the waterfront of the Cape Fear River. These occurrences went on for years and happened several times a day. As she got older and went about her own life, the occurrences gradually decreased. They are rare now.

A cousin died recently and my daughter told him to disrupt any energy field he could to let her know he was all right. It is amazing how many times her computer turned itself on and off without anyone touching it!

30
Time

Now, time, if you study it carefully, is a very strange concept. We like to perceive it as linear, a straight path delivering up history in a day-by-day fashion. Yesterday is followed by today, which becomes yesterday soon enough. Tomorrow is made anew each night at midnight and has 24 hours to exist as such.

Time is slow; time is fast. The speed at which the clock ticks depends, at least to some degree, on the mindset of the clock-watcher. Ten minutes in a dental chair, even with a speed drill, is just not the same amount of time as ten minutes spent dozing in a rocking chair. And, unfortunately, the length of a month changes unbelievably from one passed in childhood to a similar amount of time occurring much later in life.

Remember how short the summer was when we were children? And remember how very slowly the school year passed while we awaited that long-anticipated summer? The concept that time is relative is certainly something we all have experienced.

In fact, several years ago, I definitely experienced this phenomenon. I was trying to get home in a snowstorm and realized, almost as soon as I left the office, that my car was not handling the road conditions well at all. In fact, I was sliding all over the road.

Normally, I'm a pretty good driver in snowy conditions. After all, I've had a lot of years to hone my skills! And I had all-wheel drive. So I should have been fine. Wrong. Didn't happen that way. Apparently the tread on my tires would have been fine for a few thousand more miles in the flat country. But I think they just didn't have quite enough tread for the road conditions.

But, let's get back to my discussion of time. After pulling off several times on my way home because I was exhausted from trying to control the car, I finally made it to a very steep and dangerous hill near my house. I pulled off at the top and sat there for about 30 minutes gathering my courage to head down the hill. I knew that, once I started, I was committed. There would be no stopping and no turning back. That was the longest 30 minutes I had spent in quite a while.

I finally got up my nerve and headed down the hill. I made it fairly well. I slid only a tiny bit. When I got home, there was the great new parking turnaround that we had bulldozed out recently. I didn't have to make the usual get-up-speed-and-skid-up-the-driveway move that I used to do in snow.

I didn't go right in the house, though. I had to stop shaking first. I felt like I had spent many hours hovering at the top of that hill. So I can testify that time changes with one's state of mind.

But what if time were not linear at all? Or, what if time went the other way?

I love physics. Although I am pretty good at mathematics, numbers can bore me after a while. If they didn't, I might have pursued a career in physics. Practical physics falls more into "things that bore me." Theoretical physics is where I'm fascinated and could go and stay a while.

I have read books by Stephen Hawking, Brian Greene, and many others. One of them, I think it may have been Greene, speculated that our time moving forward is merely an accident of the universe; that time could have moved backward just as easily. That is mind-boggling, isn't it? Can you imagine moving from death to birth? Now that really would be becoming childlike in old age. No, wait—young age. Oh heck, one almost can't even imagine that concept.

One theory that catches my imagination is the concept of all possible worlds existing simultaneously. Hawking had a fondness for that one. Every possible action by every single person would be happening at the same time in one of these multiple universes. That would give us infinite alter egos, wouldn't it? If you subscribe to that theory, you'll be forced to wonder constantly what your other selves are doing at the moment in all those other universes. I read a science fiction novel recently where the hero met another "self" who had stepped into this world from one of the "all possible worlds" because he was seeking one he liked better. In this book, there was a threshold whereby one could enter another world if one did not like the world one was born into. And then I read another book where the author theorized that we can possibly switch between worlds if we don't like the path we are presently taking. That is a little far out there for me. But wouldn't it be fun? I could switch to the world in which I actually do win the lottery with the ticket I buy every so often.

In Hawking's theory, for every possible action at any given time, a copy of you branches off into every different scenario and lives out that life in that world. Recently, I saw where someone had made a case for immortality based on this theory. It goes something like this: suppose you die and that is only one of the possible outcomes of whatever caused you to die. So, perhaps you are dead in the life you die in. But suppose you just switched to another one of these possibilities and remained alive in all the others? And there must be at least one life in which you live forever if all possibilities are present. If we branch off into another life, does our consciousness just keep going in all the branches? It could get really confusing really quickly!

I think I like this world with its familiar trappings and somewhat predictable outcomes better. Unless you are dealing on a quantum level, of course. Then, accepted laws of physics change greatly and very strange things occur. Did I mention I love quantum mechanics?

I am always amazed when I look back and realize how much time

Time

has passed since each milestone in my life occurred.

I remember my grandmother talking about time getting faster and faster as she got older. I also remember my mother talking about how odd time was and how she felt no older on the inside no matter how much older her body got.

Time IS strange. I've always known that. Why does the time we spend in the dental chair pass so much more slowly than the time we spend visiting with friends or doing something else we enjoy?

My daughter, that gloriously beautiful toddler of just a few years ago, has turned into an adult woman who is still gloriously beautiful. How did that happen? It almost seemed like the blink of an eye!

I remember the summer after my freshman year in college when I went to Sarasota with my roommate and her parents. The entire motel was filled with retirees, or so it seemed to me. I remember looking with a kind of pity at their aged bodies and thinking I would never get that old. The years stretched out ahead of me and seemed to be a wonderful buffer, a protection of sorts from old age. Now, I'm getting too close for comfort to the same age those people probably were.

I graduated from college fifty-five years ago this very spring. No way. That can't possibly be. Maybe it has been fifteen years or so. But fifty-five? That just isn't possible.

Once, a few years ago, I experienced a very strange time. It felt like I had stumbled upon Brigadoon where time stood still and nothing worked as it was supposed to work. Let me tell you about it and you can draw your own conclusions.

Somewhere along Interstate 95 near Orangeburg, SC, I encountered a time warp. Well, it may not have been a bona fide time warp of science fiction proportions, but it was quite strange to me.

As Bruce and I exited the Interstate in search of lodging for the night, I was on the cell phone talking eagerly with Neal McLaurin, one of my favorite cousins. We were planning the next day's big visit in Wagener, the birthplace of my mother not far from Aiken.

Neal, who had the russet hair and robust coloring of the true Scotsman, was quite dear to my heart and we had not seen each other in several years.

It had been even longer since I had seen his mother, my Aunt Iris. She was one of my mother's three sisters and, although she was 88 years old at that time and had had a stroke that made her speech a bit difficult, she was doing fairly well.

Bruce and I had just come from a couple of days on Merritt Island, FL, with Mother's youngest sister, Pauline Leister. She and her husband Will were about 80 years old then. That was so hard to believe because they had not slowed down much—not physically and especially not mentally. It was Pauline who once told me she would never grow old gracefully; she would fight it every inch of the way! I'm so glad she did.

For years, every time I had a crisis or a big problem, I would hop on a plane and head to Pauline and Will's for the weekend. Pauline and I would sit up all night and talk until we were both hoarse. Maybe my problem was not solved when I left, but I always felt infinitely better. Now both of my aunts are gone and so is my cousin, but that is what time does. But I'm digressing from my story.

Anyway, as we turned onto the exit where there were several chain hotels, my phone suddenly went dead. Now I know that happens a lot, but I had a great signal and a full charge.

How strange, I thought. I figured I would call Neal back as soon as I got settled for the night.

It didn't happen that way. We checked into the Fairfield Inn and I immediately hooked up my laptop to the high speed Internet. No problem. Worked like a charm!

Having done that, I tried my cell phone again. Full signal. Full charge. No dice! What was going on?

So Bruce tried his cell phone. The very same thing happened. I also had my cell phone I use in the High Country, so I tried it. (For some unknown reason, my High County cell phone won't work in Greeneville and my Greeneville cell phone won't work in the High Country, so I have two phones.) That phone didn't work either.

Things were getting stranger by the minute. We had three cell phones with great signals and full charges and we couldn't call anyone.

We tried our homes, our offices—nothing.

Finally, after many attempts, I got through to my daughter, who was in Kentucky. Thankfully, I gave her my hotel phone number and room number. I say "thankfully," because just as soon as I gave her the numbers, the call abruptly stopped and I couldn't get her again. Interestingly, she couldn't get her cell phone to connect with ours and there were three different cell phone companies represented.

I called down to the front desk and asked the clerk if there was usually trouble getting out on cell phones. She told me that the cell phone service was wonderful around and in the hotel and that, to her knowledge, no one had ever had a problem with it. Bruce and I just looked at each other in total puzzlement for a few seconds.

A couple of minutes later, our room phone rang. It was the front desk clerk. "I had to call you back because, for the first time ever, my cell phone isn't working either, even though it has a great signal and is fully charged," she told me.

Aha! At least we weren't the only ones. Truthfully, we were wondering if we had wandered into the Twilight Zone or had been abducted without our knowledge by aliens or had stumbled into a four-block area where the usual laws of physics didn't apply. It was mystifying and more than a little creepy.

I never did get Neal again that night. However, as soon as we got back on the Interstate the next morning, our cell phones worked perfectly again. I called Neal to finish arranging the day's visit. So go figure!

We went on to Wagener and had a wonderful visit with Aunt Iris, Neal and his wife Maggie, Neal's sister Ann and her husband Phillip, and a few more Jones cousins.

But somewhere out there in a small, obscure four-block area just off Interstate 95 in the vicinity of Orangeburg, things aren't quite as they seem. I think I will drive on to Columbia next time!

31

Making Postulates

I'm sure you've heard the old adage, "Be careful what you wish for—you just might get it!" I'm also fond of the saying, "Your thoughts create your future." Since I believe that, I always try to choose the good ones!

I think it is very important to create postulates in your life. What are postulates? Postulates are statements you make about things you want in your life or events you want to happen and which you treat as though they were true. While at the time you make the postulate it is not yet true, if you act as though it were, many times it does come true!

Somewhere along the line, I got into the habit of making postulates like the following ones rather than resolutions for the coming year—I make them and act like they are true (whether they actually are or not). One good example is: My family members and I all have good health. Another is: I have an excellent job in which I can use all my skills. Or: I am bringing my estranged family members back together in good communication. Or whatever it is you really want to achieve or obtain.

Notice that I wrote the statements as though they were actually happening. I did not say, "I want to get a good job." As Dr. Wayne Dyer, psychologist and author of many books, would say—you get what you ask for and if you ask to want something, you will just keep on wanting it all year! I think that is a great point!

New Year's is a time when many people look back over the past year and try to figure out some good resolutions for the next year. Some of us (yes, I'm including myself) write down a list of the important events, births, deaths, celebrations, etc., that have occurred over the past year. I am always delighted to run across these old lists from years past. One tends to forget just when a lot of things happened. I have found similar lists I made when I was a child and then a young adult. They are pretty good reading. They included my plans for the upcoming year and I always had great plans!

Also, I didn't say, "I will get a good job." The word "will" implies the future and it may or may not find its way into the present. It is always a good thing to set a time limit on when you want these things to happen.

So, assume it is happening, act like it is true, and your subconscious will quite often find a way to make it come into being.

When you make a postulate, be sure to present a completely clear picture of exactly what you desire to come into your life. As you are formulating your postulate, hold the image of the object or the event or whatever you want clearly in your mind so your postulate can truly reflect your objective. Then be very specific. It doesn't really matter if you make big postulates or little postulates, just as long as they are simple and clearly stated.

Making a postulate is actually goal-setting. If you really pay attention, you may notice that small (or even large) incidents of synchronicity happen that will move you toward achieving your desired result. Look for any feelings or unusual coincidences that seem to just happen out of the blue. Remember that you manifest from postulates in totally unexpected ways most of the time. So don't focus your postulates on the "how." As I have said, that is not your job! You make the postulate or set the goal. God and the universe will figure out the rest!

It seems the subconscious or inner mind has a pull on or a connection with the universe that crafts everything that is our reality. Many people think the little signs of synchronicity that pop up so often are the universe's way of telling us that we are on the right path and the things we are trying to manifest are happening.

One noteworthy caution I would mention: it may not be such a great idea to share your postulates and goals with just anyone. Sometimes even close relatives and friends will tell you your ideas and desires are crazy and impossible to attain and thereby ruin any chance of successful manifesting. I've seen this result all too often. When you doubt your own abilities to obtain your goals, you sabotage your chances and work against the forces that would otherwise guide you.

I have found out something over the years—you must be careful what you wish for. For instance, you don't want to get a new car because your old one was in an accident. Frankly, I have gotten some of the things I postulated in totally unexpected ways.

One year, one of my postulates was for a new roof. I really couldn't afford a new roof that year. I had a child in college and I wasn't making much money. I have told the extended version of my new roof in Chapter 18, but let me briefly recap it here because it was not only synchronicity that happened, but also was created from my postulate. Out of the blue (seemingly), an old friend called me from Arkansas. He had a friend in Georgia who was in a rather messy divorce situation and my friend wanted to give his friend my number. I had been a therapist for many years in the past and he thought his friend could benefit from talking to me. To make a long story short, his friend did call, we spent a lot of time working through his feelings about his divorce, and he came up to North Carolina to thank me.

He was an instructor in technology at a major university and he immediately spotted my need for a new roof. He came up for several weekends and brought all the materials and equipment and put on a new roof for me. I was astounded! When I tried to pay him, he wouldn't hear of it. He said it was a very small payback for all the help I had given him over the past few months.

My new roof was nothing short of a miracle. Dr. Phyllis Crain, who was director of Crossnore School, Inc., always said we live in "Miracle Country." I quite agree.

Through the years, some of the biggest sellers in the book world have been books that claimed to give one the secret of being rich, being famous, being a no-limit person, being at ease, and on and on. I figured out that most of the books on being rich actually did make someone rich—the person who wrote the book!

But there are a lot of books that can help you feel good about yourself. My personal favorites, as I have mentioned, are the books and tapes of Dr. Wayne Dyer and Dr. Deepak Chopra. I also have found that you stay "hyped up" for only a little while and you have to keep inputting motivational stuff to stay motivated!

I get an e-mail message from "The Universe" each morning telling me a good thought for the day. This bit of fun comes from Mike Dooley, author of *Infinite Possibilities*. Today's thought said, "Yes, Nancy, you can have whatever you want. ANYTHING you can imagine. You name it. It's yours. Done deal. Oh, but you have to go get it. Okay? I'll help. The Universe." Hey, not too shabby a start to a new day, is it?

Lately, I've been reading several books on quantum physics and the strange ways in which the infinitely small world operates. I have come to visualize everything and everyone as being connected, while appearing to be separate. That view of the universe has made me more aware of our connectedness and how what affects one person can affect many others, and on a lot of different levels. Obviously some very basic connections exist on the cellular level.

At one point in my life years and years ago, I was married to a man who was very involved in Scientology. Yeah, I know what you've heard and much of it is true, at least it was for me. I did feel that Scientology's founder, the late L. Ron Hubbard (science fiction writer), borrowed heavily from psychology for his theories, but some things were interesting. One thing he emphasized was the effect of postulates and how our postulates help to determine the way our lives proceed. For me, that is not very different from "Your thoughts create your future." I always make a list of postulates every year and New Year's seems like a good time to make such a list.

However, the main thing I got from my husband's involvement in Scientology was the chance to hang out with musicians Chick Corea and Stanley Clarke for a while in Los Angeles!

In other times, I've explored many paths toward enlightenment, nirvana, etc. I've studied all the Eastern religions— Hinduism, Buddhism, Taoism, and more. I've even spent time learning from the son of a Navajo medicine man!

I have finally reached one conclusion in my search. And, surprisingly, it is exactly what I told my daughter for years when she asked me if Santa Claus were real. "If you believe, you receive." The act of believing is the key to any path you may choose.

32

Guided Meditation

Meditation gets you aligned with whatever vibratory level is needed to manifest your desires.

Meditation has been used the world over for centuries by everybody from practitioners of Eastern religions to people just wanting to relax or to sleep better. In fact, several people have told me that the more one practices meditation in order to sleep better, the better one sleeps. Meditation is the practice of getting into a comfortable position and letting your mind clear of all stress and troubling thoughts. Meditation can bring one peace of mind, relaxation, and relief from anxiety, according to its advocates. Others tout the flow of positive energy that consistent meditation seems to produce.

Meditation moves you away from unpleasant thoughts and fills your mind with positive energy. We can all use more positive thoughts and positive energy in our lives in these troublesome times. Pandemic lockdowns, mandatory masks, loss of income, fear of becoming ill or dying, and social isolation have caused so many problems. Depression and suicidal thoughts have skyrocketed, even among our schoolchildren. Drug use has increased.

Since many people sometimes have a bit of a struggle learning to clear the mind, guided meditation can be a little easier. Guided meditation is just what it sounds like: an instructor or teacher or guide talks one through an exercise that can be as short as five minutes or as long as one wants. After all, even five minutes is certainly better than no minutes! Guided meditation can keep one focused.

Many guided meditations can be found online these days and

Guided Meditation

many of them are free and downloadable. Search for keywords "guided meditation" and then the subject, such as "stress relief" or even the setting like "at the beach." You will be surprised at the wealth of meditations on a vast array of subjects that are yours for the taking.

At the end of this discussion I am including several guided meditations that I created. You certainly can create your own. Get out your tape recorder and get creative!

The actual visualization is the important part. Your meditation needs to be easily imaginable, so the setting should be a place you are familiar with or can easily picture in your mind. Keep your meditation as simple as you can.

I have read that, when visualizing, it is really important to engage as many of the senses (smell, touch, hearing, sight—in your mind's eye, texture, etc.) as you can. It is also important to be aware of your breathing.

Your position needs to be very comfortable and very relaxed. Many people report that they have trouble staying awake if they lie down to meditate. It might be best to sit fully relaxed in a comfortable chair. You will have to try both for yourself and see which one works better.

Some people listen to peaceful music while meditating. Others report that they have trouble clearing their mind when there is music. Again, whether to use music or not is a personal choice.

If you want to use the guided meditation examples I have provided here, just take a tape recorder (most mobile phones have recording capability these days) and read the meditations slowly and softly, letting your voice be as mellow and relaxing as possible. Then you can play your recording as often as you wish to help you relax.

The examples I have provided are geared toward relaxation, but if you have other goals, you can find meditations geared toward almost any goal you might desire online. (These meditations are already recorded, usually by someone with a soothing, relaxing voice!)

The first guided meditation is a walk on the beach:

Feel yourself relaxing, relaxing, relaxing. Start with your toes. Clench your toes as tight as you can. Hold: one—two—three—four—five. Slowly unclench your toes and let them relax. Next flex your ankles. Bend your feet up at the ankles. Hold: one—two—three—four—five. Slowly relax your feet. Feel the relaxation moving up your legs to your calves. Flex the muscles in your calves. Hold: one—two—three—four—five. Now slowly relax your calves. Next clench the muscles in your thighs. Hold: one—two—three—four—five. Slowly relax your thighs. Tighten your buttocks. Hold: one—two—three—four—five. Slowly relax your buttocks. Next, tighten the muscles in your stomach. Hold: one—two—three—four—five. Slowly relax your stomach muscles. Clench the muscles in your chest. Hold: one—two—three—four—five. Slowly relax the muscles in your chest. Make a tight fist with your hands. Hold: one—two—three—four—five. Slowly relax your hands. Feel the relaxation moving up your arms. Bend your wrists upward. Hold: one—two—three—four—five. Slowly relax your wrists. Bend your elbows tightly. Hold: one—two—three—four—five. Slowly relax your elbows. Shrug your shoulders. Hold: one—two—three—four—five. Slowly relax your shoulders. Now scrunch up your face, your nose, your eyes, your mouth. Hold: one—two—three—four—five. Slowly relax your face. You are very relaxed and ready to start your journey. As you continue, you will feel yourself becoming more and more relaxed and peaceful feelings fill you. You are floating, floating, floating. Walking is so easy, so effortless. You feel sunshine on your face and you lift your face toward the sun. It feels so warm. You take a minute to relax and enjoy the warm, clean feeling of the sun on your face and arms. You take a deep breath and you smell the salty, slightly fishy smell of the ocean. You feel

Guided Meditation

the gentle breeze on your face, softly blowing and lifting your hair. You breathe in the balmy air and with each breath, you relax a little more. You hear the soft roaring and receding of the ocean waves as they crash on the sand and slowly slip back into the sea. You easily walk toward the water's edge. A little wave slides over your feet and you feel the sand under your feet as the little wave recedes. You hear the sound of the seagulls and you watch as they soar and dip overhead, occasionally diving into the waves for a morsel to eat. Looking down, you see a beautiful scallop-shaped seashell lying on the smooth sand. You reach down and pick up the shell. You turn it over in your hands and see that the shell is a pinkish peach color on the inside. You run your fingers over the smooth inside of the shell and you see your life flowing smoothly like the smoothness of the shell. You put the shell in your pocket for safekeeping to take home so you will always have the reminder of the beach and the relaxation you found there. You walk farther down the beach just at the edge of the water. You feel the coolness of the water and the dampness of the sand. You take a deep breath and enjoy the feeling of peace that comes with smell of the ocean and the salty air. You continue your gentle walk along the beach, relaxing and enjoying the effortless walking until you decide you are ready to return. You can return easily at any time by counting backward from five. On the count of one, you will find yourself fully alert, at peace, and ready to take on your life again. Five—four—three—two—one!

The next guided meditation is a visit to a beautiful mountain stream. It starts out exactly like the walk on the beach, but ends up in a different place:

Feel yourself relaxing, relaxing, relaxing. Start with your toes. Clench your toes as tight as you can. Hold: one—two—three—four—five. Slowly unclench your toes and let them relax. Next flex your ankles. Bend your feet up at the ankles. Hold: one—two—three—four—five. Slowly relax your feet. Feel the relaxation moving up your legs to your calves. Flex the muscles in your calves. Hold:

one—two—three—four—five. Now slowly relax your calves. Next clench the muscles in your thighs. Hold: one—two—three—four—five. Slowly relax your thighs. Tighten your buttocks. Hold: one—two—three—four—five. Slowly relax your buttocks. Next, tighten the muscles in your stomach. Hold: one—two—three—four—five. Slowly relax your stomach muscles. Clench the muscles in your chest. Hold: one—two—three—four—five. Slowly relax the muscles in your chest. Make a tight fist with your hands. Hold: one—two—three—four—five. Slowly relax your hands. Feel the relaxation moving up your arms. Bend your wrists upward. Hold: one—two—three—four—five. Slowly relax your wrists. Bend your elbows tightly. Hold: one—two—three—four—five. Slowly relax your elbows. Shrug your shoulders. Hold: one—two—three—four—five. Slowly relax your shoulders. Now scrunch up your face, your nose, your eyes, your mouth. Hold: one—two—three—four—five. Slowly relax your face. You are very relaxed and ready to start your journey. You feel the clean mountain air swirling around your face and lifting your hair. The breeze carries the scent of the forest, the moss, the leaves, the rocks, and the trees. You look around and see that you are standing on a leaf-covered path with trees as far as you can see on both sides of the path. You walk easily and effortlessly along the path enjoying the sun peeking through the overhead canopy of leaves. As you walk, you are filled with a sense of peace and wellbeing. You hear the birds sing to each other and you watch as a bird flies through the trees near you flashing its lemon yellow wings. You watch as it flies higher and higher and finally vanishes from view into the thick forest of trees. You hear a small soft noise and a small deer with spots on its back steps softly out of the forest. The deer sees you and stops. It stands very still and looks into your eyes. The deer seems unafraid and you enjoy the sight of one of nature's beautiful creatures until it turns and slowly makes its way back into the forest. You continue to walk along the path effortlessly and easily. You take a deep breath and again smell the clean freshness of the forest and feel the gentle breeze swirl around you. You listen for a minute and then you hear another sound. This sound is a familiar one. It sounds like water flowing over rocks and you look around you for the source of the noise. Listening carefully, you can tell that the noise is just off the path to your left so you step into the forest to find the water you are hearing. You go deeper into the trees and soon you come out into a clearing and you see a beautiful mountain stream. The clean, sparkling water is flowing merrily over mossy rocks in small waterfalls as it makes its way through the forest and down the mountainside. You make your way down to the stream and kneel down beside the running water. You cup your hands in the crisp clean stream and lift your hands to your mouth to drink. The taste is pure and relaxing on your tongue. As you look into the stream, you see small fish darting and playing with one another. On a rock in the middle of the stream, there is a small black salamander with white spots sunning itself. You take a deep breath relaxing even more as you do. You sit beside the stream for as long as you want to, breathing deeply and relaxing. You feel at peace and all is well in your world. When you decide you are ready to return, you can do so easily at any time by counting backward from five. On the count of one, you will find yourself fully alert, at peace, and ready to take on your life again. Five—four—three—two—one!

The third guided meditation is about time spent in a beautiful garden:

Feel yourself relaxing, relaxing, relaxing. Start with your toes. Clench your toes as tight as you can. Hold: one—two—three—four—five. Slowly unclench your toes and let them relax. Next flex your ankles. Bend your feet up at the ankles. Hold: one—two—three—four—five. Slowly relax your feet. Feel the relaxation moving up your legs to your calves. Flex the muscles in your calves. Hold: one—two—three—four—five. Now slowly relax your calves. Next clench the muscles in your thighs. Hold: one—two—three—four—five. Slowly relax your thighs. Tighten your buttocks. Hold: one—two—three—four—five. Slowly relax your buttocks. Next, tighten the muscles in your stomach. Hold: one—two—three—four—five. Slowly relax your stomach muscles. Clench the muscles in your chest. Hold: one—two—three—four—five. Slowly relax the muscles in your chest. Make a tight fist with your hands. Hold: one—two—three—four—five. Slowly relax your hands. Feel the relaxation moving up your arms. Bend your wrists upward. Hold: one—two—three—four—five. Slowly relax your wrists. Bend your elbows tightly. Hold: one—two—three—four—five. Slowly relax your elbows. Shrug your shoulders. Hold: one—two—three—four—five. Slowly relax your shoulders. Now scrunch up your face, your nose, your eyes, your mouth. Hold: one—two—three—four—five. Slowly relax your face. You are very relaxed and ready to start your journey. As you continue, you will feel yourself becoming more and more relaxed and peaceful feelings fill you. You are walking through a meadow filled with green grass and wildflowers in blue, yellow, pink and purple. You feel the sunshine on your face and you smell the scent of the wildflowers and the white clover blossoms in the grass. You walk through the field feeling the grass slide across your feet and ankles. As you continue to walk through the field, you become more and more relaxed. Good feelings and positive energy fill your body and your mind. As you breathe in, feel yourself breathing in positive energy. As you breathe out, feel all the pain and negativity in your life flowing out with your breath. As you walk, you are filled with wellbeing and good thoughts. You come to the end of the field and there is a gate. The gate is a beautiful metal one with sculptured metal vines entwined around the posts. There is a simple latch on the gate. You lift it easily and open the gate. In front of you is a lovely garden filled with flowers of all kinds in every color. There are blue cornflowers, purple asters, yellow sunflowers, pink morning glories, daisies in yellow and white, roses in red and pink, tulips in pink, daffodils in yellow, hyacinths in purple, pansies in yellow and black, lilies in orange and pink, and many more. Everywhere you look, you see colorful flowers. As you watch, a hummingbird hovers over an orange trumpet flower and drinks its fill. Then it flies to the next flower and drinks again. You walk effortlessly through the garden among the beautiful flowers. As you walk, you feel yourself becoming more relaxed until you feel happy and serene. You feel goodness and positive energy flowing to you from all the beauty around you. You stop and smell the sweet fragrance of a lovely yellow rose. As you breathe

Guided Meditation

in the scent, you breathe in healing energy and healthy vibrations and you feel your body getting stronger and you feel happiness surrounding you in this wonderful garden. You watch as a fat little bumblebee flies to a yellow daisy and almost disappears into the center of the flower. When it climbs back out, its legs are covered with yellow pollen. It flies to another flower and dives head first into its center again. You walk on in the garden, breathing in the soothing air and feeling more and more at peace with the world. For as long as you want, you walk through the garden. When you decide you are ready to return, you can do so easily at any time by counting backward from five. On the count of one, you will find yourself fully alert, at peace, and ready to take on your life again. Five—four—three—two—one!

I hope you found one of these guided imagery sessions to be to your liking. But please give creating your own a try. It is fun and nobody knows you like you do! You really can relax in this manner. Create a spot that fits you. Look for the available *The Magic Within Journal* for a great place to record your miracles, dreams, gratitude, postulates, affirmations, and guided meditations. After you write down your meditations, record them in your own voice or have someone record them for you.

These meditations are intended to help you relax, let go of stress, and feel good about yourself. Please note that these techniques are not to be used to treat medical or emotional issues in lieu of professional help if it is needed.

33

Out of the Body Experiences

*End? I think not.
What can death be?
Is it merely a change of dimension?
Or is it a new beginning?
One night as I lay in my bed,
I suddenly found myself outside,
Looking down at my physical body.
And from that enlightening night,
My concept of death has changed,
And I have lost my fear.
The consciousness, I think, lives on.
It is quite a comforting thought.*   — Nancy Stroupe

Through the decades, many thousands of people have reported experiencing out of body (OBE) or near death (NDE) experiences. Many books have been written on the subject. Even surgeons report that many of their patients who experience clinical death, where the heart stops for a time, attest to having had such experiences while clinically dead. It is hard to disprove these experiences many times because the "dead" person reports word-for-word conversations that took place in the operating room while the surgical team was working hard trying to revive the patient.

The experiences are subjective. So far, there is no incontrovertible proof, but the person having the experience sometimes is so shaken by the incident that he is changed forever. Many people report that they are no longer afraid of death as their experience was pleasant and extremely comforting.

The poem at the beginning of this chapter is one I wrote back in late 1976 or early 1977 about an experience I had when I was living in eastern North Carolina and working as psychotherapist at a four-county mental health center, probably in 1969.

A group of us working in the area of mental health were exploring various aspects of parapsychology and related fields. We decided to take a course in astrology and found a nearby university professor who regularly taught a private course on the subject. He taught us how to set up horoscopes and how to interpret the position of the heavens and the zodiac. It was very interesting. And so was the professor who got up at 3:00 a.m. and stood on his head for several hours before going to his classes!

In that class, there was a woman and her daughter who claimed to be able to have out of the body trips together any time they chose. I was skeptical, as always, of their stories. I kept trying to find holes in their accounts or other clues that they were fabricating their "trips" together. I never found anything amiss. And it made me envious of their claimed abilities. Could I be capable of such an accomplishment? I wanted to find out.

Over a period of several weeks, I read everything I could get my hands on about astral projection, as it was called. Many writers swore astral projection was possible and they had done so, some on many occasions.

One account that I found most interesting was a book about astral projection written by Brad Steiger. As I remember it, in his book, he delineated exercises that could help one separate from the physical body. One such exercise was to lie on a bed on your back. Then try to raise your upper body from the waist up without raising your body! The theory was that at some point you would just pop on out and separate. That was a lot easier said than done! I tried and I tried. Sometimes I thought I got close, but I never did just "pop" apart. But I kept trying. Every afternoon I tried for a few minutes. Then, every night after I got in bed, I tried my exercises before I went to sleep. I gave it a month or so, but I still just couldn't do it.

One night, after I turned the lights off, I lay there for a few minutes trying to raise my upper body. My husband had drifted off to sleep and was softly snoring.

And then, I was on the ceiling! Just like that! There was my body, still lying on the bed and it looked asleep. Although there was no light in the room and it was dark, I could see. The air was strange and purplish with subtle hints of other colors. I could feel it; it was heavier than I was. If I moved my arm or hand, the air swirled almost as if I were stirring some light liquid. I could see the tiny molecules of air as they flowed around me. I sort of had a body, but it was different. It was light with no weight and I could float and drift.

Then I had a really horrible thought. In all my reading and studying about astral projection, I had never read anything about how to get back in my body! I didn't have a clue about what to do to reconnect. I panicked. Oh my gosh, was I going to have to stay disconnected forever?

Somehow I thought if I could just rouse my body sleeping on the bed, if I could make something move like my elbow or arm, then I could get back into my body. I tried and tried and finally my arm moved and I popped back in.

Later, I realized that I probably had not needed to move anything and that just the thought of getting back in and reconnecting was enough to reconnect. But that was later. At that moment, I was so incredibly relieved that I would not have to spend eternity trying to reconnect with my body.

Actually, the experience scared me so that I was reluctant to try it again even though I reassured myself that I could do it any time and easily reconnect.

I lay there for a couple of minutes thinking about my experience and marveling that I had really done such a thing. I got so excited.

I woke up my husband and told him all about what I had just done. He did not believe me. He did not believe me when I talked about the experience months and years later. He thought I was dreaming or had imagined it. I was not and I did not. I had not been to sleep! I was quite disappointed and frustrated that I could not convince him I really had experienced astral projection.

I have never tried it again. As I said, it scared me when I realized I did not know how to get back in my body.

Something else is a little strange. I remember very distinctly that I was reading information about astral projection in a book that was written by Brad Steiger. When I tried to find the exercises I had been reading about, the only book I could find by Brad Steiger on astral projection was written in 1982. I was doing these exercises in 1969. I did find a mention of a book on astral projection he had written in 1997, so possibly there was a much earlier edition of the astral projection book, but the copyright page lists only the one edition. Perhaps the exercises were in another of Steiger's books. He was a prolific writer and penned nearly 200 books. But for now, the source I was using at that time remains a mystery.

34

Negative Energy & Thoughts

Every now and then, someone tells me they are having trouble dealing with negative thoughts that interfere with their creation of positive energy, positive postulates, and positive thoughts. Certainly those individuals who tend to have obsessive-compulsive issues deal with this problem on a daily basis. Also, people who share their goals and desires with people who are not supportive and who tend to ridicule face this same problem.

We all know what negative energy feels like. It has a very depressing and detrimental effect on our feeling good and doing well. It severely limits us in every way. But getting away from negative energy is hard for those whose lives have long been filled with such negativity. In many cases, being reared in an abusive home or being in an abusive relationship can keep one in a negative energy cycle. Telling someone to "just think positive thoughts" is too simplistic. Obviously, if a person is still in the negative relationship, things have to improve before the person can experience a more positive energy flow.

The topic is a complex one and a few paragraphs here are not going to do much to help if there is a serious and long-term problem. Again, let me stress that this book is not meant to provide any sort of treatment for serious emotional issues. For that, please seek your local mental health facilities and practitioners. Your medical doctor can probably recommend local therapists who can help. This book aims to help you relax, enjoy your life more, and find more ways to better achieve your goals.

Just remember that thoughts have energy. So try to think only the good thoughts. Move on from the bad ones that have so much negative energy because they tend to sap your power to manifest

Negative Energy & Thoughts

your goals and to feel good about yourself.

Of course, the best way to counter negative energy and negative thoughts is to fill your life with more positive energy and thoughts. How do you do that?

Distraction seems to be one of the ways to lift your spirits in a hurry and get your mind to release any negative thoughts. Asking yourself distracting questions for five to ten minutes can point you in a totally different direction. Some things you can ask yourself are:

• What is the day like outside? Is there any wind? Is it hot or cold? Describe today's weather.

• How many windows are in your house? Which room has the most windows?

• Mentally see yourself in the grocery store. Go down each aisle and see yourself putting the groceries you need (or want) in your cart. Imagine yourself going through the checkout line and try to figure up how much the groceries you have put in your cart will be.

• In your mind, walk around your neighborhood. See if you can name all the streets near you.

• List as many movies that you can that have happy endings.

• List the things you would like to eat if you could have anything you wanted.

Actually do these activities. By the time you have spent five or ten minutes on these exercises, you probably will have stopped your negative thoughts.

There are many other ways to lessen negative energy and thoughts and to have more positive energy and thoughts. Actually take a walk for thirty minutes or so. Focus your attention on everything around you. Just the act of walking or exercising, if you are fine physically (it is always good to check with your doctor before undertaking any form of strenuous exercise), seems to soothe and distract the mind from negative energy and negative thoughts.

Go visit someone. But be sure the person you visit is a positive-minded person who will help you feel better.

I knew one person who wrote down all her negative thoughts on a piece of paper and, saying "I release these negative thoughts," burned the piece of paper. This technique worked really well for her.

If there is a particular thought that bothers you, take a really good look at it and counter it with the opposite and positive thinking. For instance, if a negative thought such as "I am ugly" fills your mind, counter it with "I am really attractive," or "people like me and think I am good-looking." Most of our negative thoughts about ourselves stem from problems with our self-image and usually are true only in our own mind.

One very important aspect of putting positive thoughts in your life is to avoid negative "self-talk." Don't say self-deprecating things to yourself. Not ever. We all do this undermining speech at times. Watch what you say to yourself and make sure when you hear yourself saying something negative about yourself, counter it immediately with a positive thought that takes you in the opposite direction.

Another huge way to create more positive energy in your life and less negativity is by helping others. Helping others brings you out of your self-centeredness and concentrating on others lets you both feel connected to others and less worried about your own problems. Volunteering puts things into a different prospective.

Positive energy lets us break out of our mundane lifestyle and

Negative Energy & Thoughts

achieve more abundance for ourselves. As you become more familiar with self-talk that is positive and learning to replace the negative thoughts with positive ones, the whole process will get easier and easier. You will find that, the more you concentrate on very positive things in your life, the more positive things (and experiences) you will have in your life.

Just remember, you are a divine creation and you deserve the abundance the universe wants to give you. You deserve the good things, so think the good thoughts and make the good postulates. Then keep those good thoughts coming and at the front of your mind by making wonderful, positive lists of affirmations that reinforce your positive energy.

35

Trusting Your Intuition

Learn to recognize your feelings; learn to trust them. For your feelings are the only things in this world that you can truly count on.

Have you ever had a hunch about something? A strong feeling? Ever strongly felt something was wrong when you had no logical reason for doing so? Have you ever taken a different route from the one you were planning to take on a whim and then learned there was a huge wreck you avoided? Have you ever just "known" something?

Then you have used your intuition. Intuition is the ability to know something without logical reason or conscious thought. Many people use this ability much more than they realize. Studies done with chief executive officers and leaders in the corporate world show that these executives use their gut feelings and intuition very much in making their business decisions.

Our intuition, especially once we learn to trust it, can aid us in many ways. It can keep us safe as many of us have sort of a "sixth sense" when it comes to danger or dangerous situations. It can help us make the right decisions when the choices appear to be equal but, in fact, are not.

I have known people who rely heavily on their feelings in their everyday lives. They seem to make better choices and achieve success, whereas those of us who hesitate and second-guess ourselves, don't succeed nearly so often.

On the other hand, I have used my intuition to alert me to grave personal danger. The following story is one such example and was extremely frightening to me. I am convinced my intuition saved

Trusting Your Intuition

me.

Thankfully, most people are good and harbor no ill will toward others. But we need to take some safety measures to protect ourselves against those predators who have no conscience and who don't value or respect human life. My years working in the field of mental health proved that fact to me. I met some very strange people and some who were totally amoral.

It is easy to forget, though, and find oneself in a frightening situation. I did so one day years ago in the mid-70s and I have never forgotten the incident. The world has not seemed quite as safe to me since.

I used to love to go camping and, on many weekends, my shaded silver Persian cat, Nikki, and I would take off toward adventure.

On this particular weekend, we headed out of Charlotte toward the South Carolina coast and Huntington Beach State Park, a favorite camping spot of mine. We got there late Friday afternoon and spent a pleasant Saturday relaxing and soaking up the sun. The trouble started on Sunday afternoon.

I was lying on the beach, almost dozing, reluctant to pack up and start the four-hour trek back to Charlotte, when I abruptly and very distinctly felt someone watching me. The feeling was so intense that I finally sat up and glanced around. The beach has high dunes there and, on the dune right above me, sat a large black-haired man with mirrored sunglasses who appeared to be staring directly down at me. My senses went to red alert. I felt very vulnerable and very much in danger. The man had done nothing overt at that point, but somehow I knew he was dangerous and I was in danger.

Well, his staring and my feelings creeped me out, I can tell you. I gathered my belongings and headed back to my campsite. Of course the trail went right by the stranger and I was uncomfortable as I passed him. He immediately got up and walked a few feet behind me as I headed back to my tent. I tried to be calm and to act like I wasn't concerned when he followed me. But I was scared.

As I turned off at my campsite, the man passed me and got in a black van with red flames painted down each side that was parked on the side of the road across from my tent. He opened the side door and sat watching me.

By this time, I was extremely scared and the campground was rapidly emptying out. In fact, the only nearby family was right next to me, and they were about to leave. I was sure something bad would happen to me if the family left me alone with the man in the black van. I asked them if they would stay until I loaded my tent and, when they agreed, I hurried to pack.

I smoked at that time and I emptied the can I had been using as an ashtray into a trash bag. Suddenly my subconscious flashed an alarm. Not knowing quite what was wrong, I looked at the cigarette butts I had just emptied. The butts had thin gold lines around the filters—except for one. It had a thin green ring around the filter. Menthol. I never smoked menthol cigarettes. I had not put that butt in the can. Finding that menthol cigarette butt was totally the result of my intuition kicking in. I probably would not have noticed something was wrong without my subconscious flashing me a major alarm. And, if I had not, I might not have been as aware of the danger I was in.

Someone had been in my tent while I was on the beach and I was sure it had been the man now sitting in the van.

My precious cat, Nikki, seemed to be fine, although he had been hiding under my cot. But my purse, complete with keys, driver's license, my address, etc., was sitting there in plain view. I checked and nothing was missing, but my fear ratcheted up several more notches anyway. I felt like I was in extreme danger.

I loaded the last of my equipment and my cat, thanked the family

Trusting Your Intuition

who had waited, and hopped in my car. The family pulled out. I had intended to follow closely behind them, but before I could pull onto the road, the black van fell in directly behind them, cutting me off. With no other choice, I pulled out after the van. I was so scared I was shaking. I had a really bad feeling.

There is a long dirt road out to the main road and, at one point, there is a narrow bridge. The man in the van let the family's car in front of him get a good way ahead. As we approached the bridge, the van suddenly swerved across the road, blocking it and cutting off my access.

No, I thought, you are NOT going to stop me. All my adrenaline flowed into my concentration and my determination to escape from this person I now thought might be a serial killer or, at the very least, an extremely dangerous person.

In true James Bond—or maybe it was *The Dukes of Hazzard*—fashion, I floor-boarded the accelerator, shot past him on the shoulder of the road and gunned it the remaining mile or so to the main highway. My heart was about to beat out of my chest I was so scared!

The van followed me. I sped up; he sped up. I slowed down; he slowed down. After almost two hours, he was still behind me. I kept driving. I didn't have much choice. There were no cell phones then and I didn't have a clue where a police station was in any of the towns we went through. Of course, I didn't see a policeman anywhere and I was afraid to stop and look for one.

Somewhere around Darlington or Florence, when he was stopped by a traffic light, I got a ways ahead of him and quickly pulled in behind a produce stand. I waited long after I saw him go by and, when I finally got up nerve enough to get back on the road, I took an alternate route back to Charlotte, shaking the whole way.

When I finally got home, I immediately told the management at my apartment complex about the situation and they changed my locks. But I still worried for several months about what I think of as my narrow escape from a serial killer. I am absolutely convinced that, had I gotten close to that black van and the man driving it, I would never been seen alive again.

That experience stopped my camping alone forever. I haven't gone alone in all the years since. If I have to travel alone, I pick a nice, safe motel. I watch the people around me and I check exits for bushes and other dangerous areas, especially at night. If my car is a distance away, I find someone to accompany me as far as my car.

And, oh yes, as soon as the concealed carry law for handguns was enacted, I took the course. I also learned a lot more than I already knew about shooting a gun and I took self-defense courses.

Those precautions are good, I think, but the thing that saved me during that traumatic incident was purely and simply my intuition. Without my gut feeling that I was in danger, I might not have taken the steps I needed to take in order to save myself.

I have found that the more I use my intuition, and pay attention to my hunches, the better they get. The old adage that I have quoted before here is so true: what you concentrate on expands. If you are thinking about your intuition and reading (which I certainly recommend as there are many books out there about intuition) more about the subject, you will find your intuition will give you feelings about all kinds of things. The key is to listen. Otherwise, you will miss hints and clues from one of life's most amazing gifts.

36

Been There, Done That!

Déjà vu is a French word that means feeling that one has lived through the present situation before. It literally means, "already seen."

Have you ever felt as though you are repeating an action that is so very familiar you are sure you have done this action, had this conversation, or been in this place before—and yet you know you have not? Then you have experienced *déjà vu*.

My daughter recounts a story that happened to her when she visited friends a few years ago. She had never been to their house, but as soon as she saw the outside, she could describe in detail the inside rooms in the house. And she was totally correct, she learned, as soon as she entered the house.

Scientists and the medical profession have mixed opinions on the subject of *déjà vu*. Some professionals link the experience to the temporal lobe and feel the *déjà vu* experience is tied somehow into the long- or short-term memory. While there is no conclusive agreement on how common the phenomenon is, probably 60 to 80 percent of the population has experienced *déjà vu*.

Most scientists view *déjà vu* as a sort of brain glitch or a false memory generated perhaps by something in the present situation that is similar enough to a previous experience that the brain builds it into a false memory. Another suggestion is that, instead of taking the long way around to long-term memories, the brain incorporates the present situation into a memory, but sends it straight into the long-term memory banks where it is thought to be an old memory, but is in fact a memory from just a few seconds earlier.

These theories sound somewhat plausible, even if a bit fantastical. I have experienced the *déjà vu* phenomenon over my lifetime in a number of situations. I have never known quite what to make of these events. They do seem very real and they are quite puzzling. I have heard conversations where I knew exactly what was going to be said for big parts of the conversation. I have seen places I knew very well although I had never been there before. Most puzzling of all, I have been homesick for places I have never been. Of course, I do have synesthesia (crossed senses), so maybe that accounts for some of the oddities!

I have participated in some past life regressions (PLR) and those experiences were fun, but I was never sure how much was my imagination. I even did PLR with Linda Backman under the auspices of Dr. Michael Newton, who wrote one of the main books on the subject and has regressed many, many people. However, the most vivid regression I had was one I experienced entirely on my own.

I am a lover of bagpipes. Really. I can hear bagpipes and they make me cry. I can describe the feeling I get only as extreme homesickness. (And I'm not even sure for what I'm homesick!) I remember embarrassing my husband one time when I walked into the Grandfather Mountain Highland Games. There were three pipe bands playing in different areas of the field. I promptly burst into tears and I could not explain why. I just felt this really intense and painful longing. I was so homesick. It has been that way since I was a little girl.

I have never known where these feelings came from. Most of my family background is not Scottish. From where did all the familiarity and love of everything Scottish come? I had never even visited in Scotland. How could I love it so?

My judgment is still out on past lives, even though I have "remembered" many instances, both under hypnosis and in other ways. I also have a great imagination! So who knows?

Been There, Done That!

But the past-life flashback I had one night in my own living room makes me wonder. I was listening to Scottish music, I think it was the Black Watch pipe band playing "Scotland the Brave."

Suddenly, I was no longer in my living room. I was on the outskirts of a small, dirty village in Scotland, dressed in a kilt and telling my wife and two little girls goodbye as I marched off to war to fight for Bonnie Prince Charlie. My name was Colin McCallum and I knew I probably would never see my family again. It was an awful bittersweet time and my heart was heavy, but to fight was a debt I had to pay. The vision, which seemed more like a hologram, felt very real. It was over in several minutes, but I sat there stunned for quite a while. Past life? Imagination? Who knows? But it certainly would explain the feelings of homesickness I always get when I hear bagpipes, wouldn't it?

37

Using Affirmations to Help Create Your World

There are many people, including psychotherapists and even New Age philosophers, who believe in the power of positive affirmations. Affirmations are positive statements that serve to remind us that we have strengths and so motivate us to display a positive attitude and live in a powerful manner. They help our brains to attain success in whatever endeavor our affirmations lead us.

The following is a list of a few affirmations that have been used for years to motivate people in all walks of life:

- I am a big success in my career.
- Money is flowing to me from many directions.
- My health gets better and better every day.
- Being healthy is my right.
- I have much love in my life.
- I deserve money.
- I always have money for everything I want.
- I have plenty of energy.
- I deserve to be happy.
- Good things are coming to me.
- I am very smart.
- I am very handsome (pretty).
- I am good at manifesting.
- I have fun every day.
- My life is filled with abundance.
- I am powerful.
- I can do anything I want to do.
- I attract money.

Using Affirmations to Help Create Your World

- Things I want flow to me easily and effortlessly.
- I am very healthy.
- I am very happy.
- I have wonderful and fulfilling relationships.
- I accomplish everything I desire.

The list of affirmations is actually endless. They can be about anything you want to pull in or achieve. The affirmations I just listed are pretty general. You can make specific affirmations that cover your own needs and desires just as easily. Repeating your affirmations is a very good way to keep yourself goal-focused with your own motivational strategies. If you have something you want to accomplish, draw up ten or so affirmations relevant to achieving your goal and repeat them out loud (so your subconscious mind hears them and does its work) a couple of times a day.

I once had a friend who developed kidney cancer and she wanted to supplement her surgery and chemotherapy with positive healing affirmations. She made up a list of affirmations that she used for several months. She felt her affirmations sort of completed her three-prong treatment with the surgery and the chemo. The mind is a powerful tool. I'm certainly not claiming a cure for cancer here! But if she felt it helped, it probably did! It certainly didn't hurt!

Affirmations are positive-energy statements that are good to use in overcoming any negative thoughts or energy. Affirmations are truly powerful and can help immensely with your manifesting of your desires. When you use affirmations on a daily basis, self-empowerment and more positive thinking seem to flow all through your life.

38

The Magic Within

I hope you have found some points to ponder with my true stories of miracles that have happened in my life and in the lives of those around me. I am not a scientist dwelling on mathematical probabilities or someone intent on finding ways to prove that miracles can and do happen.

My life experiences have made me a believer in the connectedness of the universe and, indeed, of every living being.

I feel that life itself is intelligent and can be trusted to point us in the correct direction if we can but interpret the messages.

Many of us encounter negative energy and emotions on a daily basis and life cannot be enjoyed under such circumstances. Left unchecked, negative emotions can wreck our lives and destroy our emotional well-being. There are many ways to overcome this negativity. One can use positive affirmations, meditation, positive self-talk, quiet walks, exercise, positive imaging, community volunteer service, and other techniques.

Trusting our feelings and believing in ourselves are two of the best ways to heal and move forward, especially if there are positive affirmations flowing back to you from those around you, from your work, or from your community involvement.

Where do I stand on synchronicity? I cannot possibly deny that it is real. I don't know how it happens or why. Is it, as many people believe, the hand of God guiding us in our daily life? For me that explanation is as good as any. The true stories I've presented exhibit some pretty big odds against the theory of a random universe, don't they?

I think one of the hardest things after we accept that these events are not random is figuring out the messages we are being given. We are being shown the connectedness of the universe in so many ways. For each of us, the interpretation will be different and I think we probably have to figure it out on our own.

Is the event giving us an affirmation of something that we needed to know and for which we were seeking an answer? Is it a warning or a red flag sent to protect us from upcoming danger? Is it a sign that we are headed in the wrong direction and we need to change things?

I have heard some of my very creative friends say they don't have a clue how they came up with their creations. I have often felt the same way about my paintings. Maybe I have an idea in my head when I start, but sometimes the end result is entirely different from the project I started out to create and I have no idea how on earth that happened! I have often wondered if I am channeling my painting from perhaps the universal consciousness or non-local mind, if there is such a thing. Many times I really surprise myself. Sometimes I think, wow, how did I do that? I'm sure many of you have felt the same way.

I have to tell you that this book almost wrote itself. It flowed so easily and so rapidly. The stories were already in my mind and a few of them were already on paper and just had to be expanded. I did most of the work on the book during a six-week time period! Things just fell into place. It was meant to be!

I also have found that when I am concentrating on synchronicity and other miracles, I seem to pull in more. Eastern and New Age philosophers say what you concentrate on expands and it is true for me. There are some useful techniques that may increase your experiencing these miracles.

Just as I do to increase my memory of my dreams, I find journaling and writing down any coincidences or strange events or incidents of synchronicity seem to increase their frequency in my life. I keep a pad and a pencil handy so I can record the instances.

I also have found that, if you are seeking specific answers or advice, ask specific questions. Since you are trying to engage your subconscious mind to help you find answers, make sure that part of your brain actually hears the question. You can do that by asking your questions out loud. Be as detailed as you possibly can.

Another way to increase the synchronicity in your life is to use affirmations. You can tell yourself things like, "miracles keep appearing in my life and I notice when they happen" or "thank you for making extraordinary things happen in my life."

These miracles or incidents of synchronicity are perhaps a little deeper than just traditional cause and effect.

I have another thought, or perhaps it is a theory. You know how there is a whole range of sounds outside our range of hearing just as there is a whole range of colors beyond those colors visible to our own eyes? And there are smells dogs can smell that we can't? And radar echoes bats can decipher that we can't? What if the synchronicity of the universe is just one more thing that is logically explainable if we just had the tools to understand it? Maybe things are revealed to us on a need-to-know basis. Wouldn't it be amazing if we one day figured it out? Well, we'll see, won't we?

Until then, I think we'd better let the big guy upstairs handle things. I'm sure He does a better job than we ever could!

You might like to grab a copy of *The Magic Within Journal*, which is a companion book to this one. It will help you document your own miracles, synchronicities, dreams, and things for which you feel gratitude.

Thank you so much for sharing my journey into the world of synchronicity and other miracles. We are all gifted and enchanted

The Magic Within

beings and there truly is magic within!

Best wishes,
Nancy

P.S. I would love to hear about your incidents of synchronicity and other miracles and/or miraculous events. I might even write a sequel to this book and include your story. Please write to me at:

Timeless Treasures
P.O. Box 278
Crossnore, North Carolina 28616
or email me at: nstroupe@charter.net.

Also, if you enjoyed this book, I would really appreciate your leaving a review of this book on Amazon. It makes a difference!

Suggested Reading List

The following authors are ones I have enjoyed following through the years. I have listed several books for each, but any of their books are well worth reading. This list is only a beginning. There is a wealth of knowledge out there for the taking. Do online searches for key words such as: manifesting, synchronicity, lucid dreams, affirmations, etc. You will find more books than you could read in a lifetime! Enjoy the ride!

Wayne Dyer: *You'll See It When You Believe It, I Can See Clearly Now, Gifts From Eykis, Real Magic: Creating Miracles, Manifest Your Destiny, Excuses Begone!: How to Change, Your Erroneous Zones* and many more.

Deepak Chopra: *How to Know God, Ageless Body/Timeless Mind, Creating Affluence, Reinventing the Body, Boundless Energy, Life After Death*, and many more.

Stephen Hawking: *A Brief History of Time, The Grand Design, The Universe in a Nutshell, Black Holes and Baby Universes*, and many more.

Brian Greene: *The Elegant Universe, Until the End of Time, The Fabric of the Cosmos, The Hidden Reality*, and many more.

Michio Kaku: *Physics of the Impossible, The God Equation, The Future of Humanity, Parallel Worlds*, and many more.

Michael Newton: *Journey of Souls, Destiny of Souls, Life Between Lives*, and more.

David Wilcock: *The Synchronicity Key, The Source Field Investigations, The Ascension Mysteries*, and more.

Mike Dooley: *Infinite Possibilities, Notes from the Universe, Manifesting Change*, and more.

Jack Canfield: *Chicken Soup for the Soul, The Success Principles, The Power of Focus*, and more.

Rhonda Byrne: *The Secret, The Magic, The Power*, and more.

Napoleon Hill: *Think and Grow Rich, The Master Key to Riches, The Law of Success in Sixteen Lessons*, and more.

Nancy Stroupe

Nancy Stroupe grew up in the North Carolina High Country. Her mother taught English and Latin. Her father was Nationwide Insurance Company's first field underwriter. She graduated from Newland High School, where she was valedictorian of her class, head cheerleader, and editor-in-chief/business manager of her high school yearbook. Nancy graduated from St. Andrews University with a degree in psychology and sociology and did her graduate work at the University of North Carolina at Chapel Hill. She was a social worker with Scotland County DSS, a counselor in mental health in Robeson County, senior therapist at the Alcoholic Rehabilitation Center in Butner, North Carolina, and was director of therapeutic services and director of the long-term care unit at the Charlotte Detox. She also owned Goodman Entertainment & Events in Charlotte and booked musical entertainment on the east coast for many years. She moved to Avery County in 1994 to care for her ailing father. She became manager for the *Avery Mountain Times* and then publisher/editor for the *Avery Journal-Times* and *All About Women* magazine. When she retired from publishing, she reinvented herself as an artist in a field she always loved.

Nancy has served on and headed dozens of boards in Avery County. She also organized a six-month campaign and established two K-9 units for the Avery County Sheriff's Office; she worked with the SBI, local law enforcement and the NC Attorney General's Office to rid Avery County of local governmental corruption; was instrumental in passing the "No Felon For Sheriff" statute in N.C.; spearheaded efforts that resulted in Drug Treatment Court for Avery and Watauga counties; was elected to the Hall of Legends in 2015; was voted Woman of the Year in 2013; received Outstanding Service Award from Chamber of Commerce in 2010; received the Distinguished Service Award from Mayland Community College in 2008, and has won numerous awards from the N.C. Press Association, including Best Column, Investigative Reporting, and Community Service.

A Timeless Treasures Publication.

www.ingramcontent.com/pod-product-compliance
Lightning Source LLC
Chambersburg PA
CBHW071201160426
43196CB00011B/2153